MAKE-AHEAD
Entertaining

Mable & Gar Hoffman

·Contents·

ANOTHER BEST-SELLING VOLUME FROM HPBooks®

Executive Editor: Rick Bailey
Editorial Director: Elaine R. Woodard
Editor: Carroll P. Latham
Art Director: Don Burton
Book Design & Assembly: Leslie Sinclair
Typography: Cindy Coatsworth, Michelle Carter
Director of Manufacturing: Anthony B. Narducci

Published by HPBooks, Inc.
P.O. Box 5367, Tucson, AZ 85703   602/888-2150
ISBN 0-89586-362-6
Library of Congress Catalog Card Number 85-80246
©1985 HPBooks, Inc.   Printed in the U.S.A.
1st Printing

Mable and Gar Hoffman, HPBooks' best-selling cookbook team, have added *Make-Ahead Entertaining* to their long list of successful cookbooks. Five of Mable's seven cookbooks, published by HPBooks, have won R. T. French Tastemaker Awards, the "Oscar" for cookbooks.

In 1975, Mable authored *Crockery Cookery*, a Tastemaker-Award winner, which has sold over five million copies. Next came *Crepe Cookery*, also a Tastemaker-Award winner, followed by *Deep-Fry Cookery* and *Chocolate Cookery*. In 1980, Mable won another Tastemaker Award for *Appetizers*. Gar and Mable co-authored *Ice Cream* (1981) and *California Cooking* (1983), both Tastemaker-Award winners.

Mable and Gar make their home in Southern California where they are famous for their entertaining skills. Nothing delights them more than inviting family and friends over for planned or impromptu get-togethers. Besides developing recipes for their own books, they are actively engaged in creating delightful dishes for many commercial food firms. Mable does food styling for HPBooks and other food companies with Gar assisting on the sidelines. Together, they own and manage Hoffman Food Consultants.

The Make-Ahead Plan

Make-Ahead Entertaining is designed for today's lifestyle. Everyone is busier than ever with demanding jobs, community or political projects, family activities, sports and fitness programs, as well as other less exciting events. Getting together with friends is always an important pastime, but sometimes becomes a chore when it's your turn to entertain. It's no fun to be out in the kitchen getting dinner when everyone else is in the living room enjoying the party. If you're relaxed and enjoying yourself, everyone else is able to follow your example and have fun, too. That's when a make-ahead plan can come to your rescue. Choose the menu that appeals to you. Check the plan to see what dishes can be made ahead or what short-cuts you can take. Then several days, weeks or months early, when there's a lull in your schedule, make parts of the menu.

Although each menu in this book is complete, we know that you're likely to substitute one of your favorite foods for one that we've suggested. Or, you might choose one of our chocoholic desserts instead of the one designed for your dinner. If you're more adventurous, you may want to design your own menu by mixing and matching dishes from several of our menus. Also, with a busy schedule, you're likely to be a midnight cook while another person will make ahead most of the food on the morning before a party. *That's why we did not prepare a minute-by-minute countdown for make-ahead entertaining. In each recipe, we've told you how to prepare it ahead, how to store the food, and how to finish the dishes for serving.* We hope you enjoy the versitility this plan.

The key to using these menus is flexibility. We designed the Make-Ahead Plans to give you a wide range of time that would fit into your individual lifestyle. We realize that a rigid timetable does not fit into today's busy world.

We hope you will take some of our suggestions for short-cuts. No longer are people embarrassed to admit that they purchase quality prepared items from the bakery, deli or gourmet food shop. Some of the short-cuts produce slightly different results, but will provide you more time for other activities.

The key to successful make-ahead entertaining is careful planning. After you've decided to entertain, the next step is to develop a plan of action. Will it be a traditional breakfast, lunch or dinner, or will you have a dessert get-together, an appetizer buffet, or picnic in the park? Will it be a buffet or a sit-down affair where everyone is served? Naturally, all of these decisions depend on the number of guests, seating space, size of table and whether you have any kitchen help.

Plan your guest list. Do you prefer small intimate dinners with a maximum of two or three guests at a time? Or would you enjoy the opportunity of bringing a wide variety of interests and personalities together on the same evening?

You'll need to make that decision—then make the guest list. The total number of people you invite determines the type of entertaining, the actual menu and the equipment needed to do the job. Also decide how to invite your guests. Whether you invite guests by telephone or by written invitation, it's a good idea to indicate whether you're serving only coffee and dessert or a complete dinner. This will ensure that the guests' appetites match your supply of food.

Buffet or Sit-Down Meals—Most of us can entertain more guests by serving buffet-style. The average dining table seats about 8 people comfortably. Some tables can be extended to seat 12, but require a large dining room. On the average dining table, you can easily arrange a buffet for 12 and sometimes even 18 to 20 people, depending on the menu. At a buffet, arrange everything so guests can help themselves conveniently. Cut food into individual portions for ease in handling and assemble proper serving utensils for each dish. The disadvantage of a buffet is that guests must find a place to sit and eat. To avoid the awkward problem of balancing a plate on a knee while eating, set up card tables or snack tables to make everyone more comfortable and relaxed.

A sit-down dinner is usually slightly more formal. You'll set the table in a more traditional style with a place setting for each person. You have a choice of several ways to actually serve the food. You may choose to fill individual plates at the table or pass serving dishes, for everyone to help himself family-style. If you have kitchen help, or don't mind spending extra time in the kitchen, arrange food on individual plates in the kitchen and bring them to the table ready to eat.

Deciding on the Menu—The menu depends on the type of party. You may want to choose foods that are associated with certain holidays or special events. Don't be afraid to break tradition and combine foods that aren't usually served at the same meal. Sometimes a menu is more exciting if it combines foods from two ethnic groups rather than a complete feature of one.

Food that looks good usually tastes good. That's why it's important to think about the beauty of your food when you're planning the menu. To make it more exciting, include a variety of textures, colors and shapes, as well as compatible flavors.

Carefully check each recipe to determine all the equipment needed to prepare and serve the food. Are you missing any large pans, bowls, trays or platters? Perhaps a good friend or neighbor will lend them to you. If not, check the yellow pages for a place to rent what you need. In the case of make-ahead entertaining, especially for a large affair, you'll probably need extra refrigerator or freezer space, so be sure you plan for it.

Try unfamiliar recipes ahead of time. It's less embarrassing to serve your family something less than perfect than to try a new recipe the day of the party and find that it does not turn out as you expected. When trying a new recipe, adjust seasonings to your taste, and cooking method to your style. Write down changes you think are important so you'll remember to make it your way when preparing it for guests.

Check with your supermarket, bakery, delicatessen, meat market or any store where you plan to purchase food for the party. Make sure that all the fruits and vegetables are in season and that your favorite brands of staples are available. If certain cuts of meat or quantities of fruits must be ordered, let the store know in time to order it.

Storing Food—Cold foods should be kept below 40F (5C). Hot foods must be kept above 140F (60C) to prevent food poisoning. We'll talk more about keeping foods hot later.

Make maximum use of your freezer and refrigerator. They are your two most important helpers when you're making-ahead. Decide which recipes you'll make first. Many foods, such as breads, cookies, cakes and certain main dishes, may be made and frozen a month or so before the event. In the Make-Ahead Plans, we have listed the menu items in order of how long they can be stored. Be sure you save space in the freezer for all the foods that must be frozen.

Although the home freezer is a wonderful time-saving appliance, food from a freezer can't be any better than food that is put in the freezer. For that reason, make sure you are satisfied with the quality of food before you freeze it.

Most important, be sure food is properly packaged for freezing. Improper packaging results in freezer burn—food that is dry and unpalatable.

Regular plastic film is adequate for covering food for a day or two in a refrigerator. But for long-time freezing, use packaging material designed for that purpose. Supermarkets and hardware stores usually have special plastic freezer film and bags. Other freezer wrap and heavy-duty foil are handy for freezing, but must be sealed properly to prevent loss of moisture. When wrapping foods for freezing, press out as much air as possible and wrap tightly. If a number of servings are packaged together, such as a stack of crepes or meat patties, place a square of waxed paper or foil between each serving so you can remove the number you need without thawing the whole batch. Round or square rigid plastic containers with tight-fitting lids make handy containers for sauces, ice cream and fragile foods that may crush easily. When shopping for these packaging materials, read the labels to be sure they are designed for freezing.

Seal packages securely with freezer tape that is especially made for use in sub-zero temperatures. Masking tape will loosen in the freezer. Label each package before you freeze it. In addition to the date and name of the recipe, tell whether the food is uncooked, partially cooked or ready to eat.

In your refrigerator, you'll need space for fresh foods in addition to any recipe you make ahead. Packaging materials are not as important in a refrigerator as in a freezer because food is stored for a much shorter time. Even so, frost-free refrigerators have a tendency to dry out food. For this reason, cover all refrigerated food with foil or plastic wrap unless the storage container has a tight-fitting lid of its own. Covered food is not likely to impart or pick-up foreign odors and flavors from other foods.

During your party, if your refrigerator is bulging and there's no room for a salad or cold drinks, put ice chests to work. They don't have to be fancy. Use the inexpensive styrofoam kind or bring out the one you take camping. If it doesn't look too good, hide it in the kitchen or just outside the kitchen door. Use artificial ice if there's a shortage of ice cubes. Speaking of ice cubes, don't forget to make them ahead and keep them in an ice chest during the party. If the weather is hot, you'll need more ice, so plan accordingly.

Although much of the chopping and mixing can be done ahead of time, some foods must be assembled, heated or cooked at serving time. We have indicated in each recipe the most practical and time-saving method. For example, we suggest you partially or completely cook certain vegetables or main dishes; then reheat them just before serving. If another method is more convenient for you, use it.

We find that the broiler and oven are handy for heating food at the last minute. You can prepare a main dish or hot appetizer the day before. Put it in the oven just before guests arrive so it will be the proper temperature when you're ready to serve. With some foods, broiling is preferred because it seldom takes more than five minutes and produces appetizing foods that are bubbly hot.

A skillet, sauté pan or steamer are tools for heating sauces or vegetables. They provide a slower, more relaxed method of reheating foods, such as rice, vegetables and pastas.

Microwaving is the fastest and one of the most practical ways to heat make-ahead food. Unlike a regular oven, the time needed to heat food in a microwave depends on the quantity, as well as the density and shape of the food. In general, ovenproof glass, ceramic dishes, oven cooking bags, frozen-food pouches and most plastic dishes may be used for heating foods in the microwave. Although there's no exact formula for heating time, the microwave will heat most food in about one-fourth the time of a conventional oven.

Now that you have succeeded in bringing hot foods to the table at the preferred temperature, your next problem is to keep them hot. This is especially important when you're having a buffet and would like the last person in line to enjoy the same hot food as the first person. Here are our favorite ways to keep food hot:

Chafing dishes or fondue pots have been popular with caterers for many years. If you have either packed away in a closet or garage, get it out and put it to work. They are made in a variety of sizes and materials. Most of them will look nice on any serving table.

Hot trays are available in sizes ranging from a small square for a coffee server to the large buffet size that accommodates several serving dishes or platters. They're electric, but automatically maintain just enough current to keep foods warm.

Electric slow-cookers are often overlooked because we associate them with the actual cooking process. They are ideal for keeping soups, stews, hot drinks, hot dips, meat balls and endless other foods hot. They also keep foods hot a long time after they're unplugged. For your next picnic, fill a slow-cooker with hot baked beans. Cover it; then wrap it in several layers of newspapers. You'll be amazed how long it stays hot without electricity.

Electric skillets are handy for last-minute cooking or reheating and can be used to keep food warm at the serving table. When set on low, they give even heat for an indefinite length of time.

Conventional ovens are most likely to be used to cook food, but are also handy for keeping foods warm. This is especially true for a fairly large party or open house where you have an extra loaf of hot bread or an extra platter of meat.

Wines & Other Beverages—We have not listed beverages in the menus unless they are unique to that particular theme. We assume that you will serve coffee, tea or milk according to your custom and your guests' taste.

Entire books have been written on the subject of selecting and serving wine with foods. Not long ago, it was considered fashionable, in fact almost mandatory, to serve specific wines with specific foods. Fortunately, that tradition is no longer in vogue. Today the "right" wine is one that pleases your palate. For this reason we are not providing specific wines for the respective menus.

It is well to consider that wine and food should complement each other. The wine should not overpower the food and vice versa. The temperature at which the wine is served is also an important consideration. We feel white and rosé wines are most enjoyable at 50F (10C), red wines at 60F (15C), and sparkling wines at 40F to 45F (5C).

Ethnic wines served with the same-ethnic food is a good guide to observe in selecting wines. In most cases, these wines have been developed and refined over many centuries to complement a specific region's cuisine. Therefore, observing this premise will almost always provide a harmonious blending of flavors.

Freezing Timetable

Although some of these foods may be frozen longer, we found that many of them begin to deteriorate when kept longer than we suggest. When planning for Make-Ahead Entertaining, you will not need to store food longer than two or three months at 0F (−32C). Thawing and reheating times will vary according to size of item and temperature used for heating.

Food	Maximum Freezing Time	Comments
Cookies	2 to 3 months	Freeze 1 layer at a time on a baking sheet. When firm, wrap airtight in freezer wrap. Thaw, unwrapped, at room temperature.
Meat, Fish & Poultry Dishes	1 to 6 months	Wrap cooked meat, fish and poultry dishes in freezer wrap; freeze 1 or 2 months. Wrap and freeze uncooked meats 3 to 6 months. All should be thawed, wrapped, in the refrigerator; then used right away.
Breads & Coffee Cakes	1 to 3 months	Thoroughly cool baked breads and cakes before wrapping airtight in heavy foil or freezer wrap. Freeze cakes up to 2 months and breads up to 3 months. Thaw baked products in wrapper at room temperature. Unwrap and heat in a 350F (175C) oven.
Cakes	1 to 2 months	Freeze single-layer cakes or frosted layer cakes on a baking sheet. When firm, wrap airtight in freezer wrap. Thaw, unwrapped, at room temperature.
Pies	1 to 2 months	Wrap and freeze unbaked pastry shells, baked or unbaked single- or double-crust fruit pies. Bake while still frozen, but allow extra baking time.
Foods That Do Not Freeze:		Salad greens, uncooked tomatoes, cucumbers, cooked egg whites, mayonnaise, cake frostings made with egg whites, molded salads and meringue pies should not be frozen.

New Year's Eve Open House

Appetizer Cheesecake
Honey-Mustard Ribs
Turkey-Avocado Mousse
Bite-Size Vegetables
Salmon Spectacular
Chicken-Bacon Roll-Ups
Cheese & Jalapeño Spread
Chocolate-Hazelnut Chiffon Cake
Champagne (at midnight)

*I*t's the most exciting night of the year—time for a gala open-house celebration! Share the departure of the old year and beginning of the new with good friends whose spirits are buoyed by this special night. Bring out your best china, your most elegant table decorations and an impressive array of buffet foods.

Plan the party large enough to be festive, yet manageable. You should have something for everyone—light snacks for those who've already celebrated with an early dinner, and hearty dishes for those expecting lots of festive food.

Throughout the evening, have an open bar set up for guests to enjoy. Serves 12 to 15 people.

MAKE-AHEAD PLAN:

- **Chocolate-Hazelnut Chiffon Cake**—Bake and freeze up to 1 month ahead. Unwrap; thaw at room temperature. Glaze thawed cake.
- **Honey-Mustard Ribs**—Bake and freeze ribs up to 2 weeks ahead. Thaw in refrigerator. Marinate 1 hour; then broil.
- **Chicken-Bacon Roll-Ups**—Assemble and freeze up to 2 weeks ahead. Thaw in refrigerator.
- **Appetizer Cheesecake, Cheese & Jalapeño Spread and Turkey-Avocado Mousse**—Make each of these up to 24 hours ahead.
- **Salmon Spectacular**—Poach and refrigerate up to 24 hours ahead. Make garnishes up to 24 hours ahead; store in a plastic bag in refrigerator. On day of party, skin salmon, glaze with topping; decorate with garnishes up to 3 hours ahead.

Short-Cuts:

- Omit 1 or 2 dishes.
- Substitute plain cream cheese for the cheese spread in Cheese & Jalapeño Spread.
- Purchase or make guacamole dip; substitute for Turkey-Avocado Mousse.

Chicken-Bacon Roll-Ups

It's the kind of morsel you want to keep on eating.

2 cups cubed cooked chicken
1 egg
1 tablespoon minced fresh parsley
1 teaspoon soy sauce
1 teaspoon lemon juice

1 tablespoon chopped green onion
1/2 teaspoon Dijon-style mustard
1/2 cup soft bread crumbs
1/2 cup finely chopped water chestnuts
16 bacon slices (about 1 lb.)

In a blender or food processor fitted with a metal blade, combine chicken, egg, parsley, soy sauce, lemon juice, green onion and mustard. Process until almost smooth. In a large bowl, combine chicken mixture, bread crumbs and water chestnuts. Shape into 32 (2" x 3/4") logs. Preheat oven to 400F (205C). Cut bacon slices in half crosswise. Wrap a half-slice, in a spiral design, around each chicken roll. Arrange chicken rolls, in a single layer, in a broiler pan. Bake in preheated oven 20 to 25 minutes or until bacon is crisp. *Complete now or make ahead.*

To complete now, drain on paper towels. Arrange on a platter; serve immediately.

To make ahead, place baked roll-ups in a single layer on a baking sheet. Freeze; wrap airtight in freezer wrap or heavy foil. Store in freezer up to 2 weeks; thaw in refrigerator. Or, cool baked roll-ups 30 minutes at room temperature. Cover with foil or plastic wrap; refrigerate up to 24 hours. To reheat thawed or refrigerated roll-ups, 10 minutes before serving, preheat broiler. Place roll-ups on a broiler pan; broil about 5 inches from heat, 3 to 4 minutes or until bubbly. Drain on paper towels; serve as directed above. Makes 32 appetizer servings.

Honey-Mustard Ribs

Mustard teams well with honey for prize-winning ribs.

3 to 3-1/2 lbs. pork spareribs,
  halved crosswise
1/3 cup Dijon-style mustard
1/3 cup honey
2 tablespoons lemon juice
1/4 cup red-wine vinegar

1/3 cup lightly packed brown sugar
1 tablespoon soy sauce
1 teaspoon salt
1/4 teaspoon pepper
2 tablespoons sesame seeds
Parsley sprigs, if desired

Cut ribs into individual riblets. Place on a rack in a broiler pan. Cover with foil. Place in a cold oven. Turn oven to 325F (165C). Bake 1 to 1-1/2 hours or until meat is tender but not falling off bone. In a small saucepan, combine mustard and honey. Stir in lemon juice, vinegar, brown sugar, soy sauce, salt and pepper. Heat, stirring constantly, until sugar dissolves. Place baked ribs in a shallow bowl; pour marinade over ribs. *Complete now or make ahead.*

To complete now, cover with foil or plastic wrap; marinate in refrigerator at least 1 hour. Drain ribs 15 minutes, reserving marinade. Preheat broiler. Place ribs in broiler pan; broil 5 to 6 inches from heat, 2 to 3 minutes, brushing with marinade once. Turn; brush with marinade again. Broil 2 to 3 minutes or until browned and crisp. Place broiled ribs on a large platter; sprinkle with sesame seeds. Garnish with parsley, if desired; serve hot.

To make ahead, cool and cover with foil. Refrigerate overnight or freeze up to 2 weeks. Thaw ribs overnight in refrigerator. Drain ribs 15 minutes, reserving marinade. Preheat broiler. Broil, garnish and serve ribs as directed above. Makes 12 to 15 appetizer servings.

New Years' Eve Open House

Make Salmon Spectacular the center of attention on your gala table. Surround it with a variety of our elegant cold dishes. Occasionally, add one of the hot dishes. When the midnight bells toll, be prepared to pop the champagne for everyone to toast the new year!

Salmon Spectacular, page 14

Cheese & Jalapeño Spread

This combination is so delicious and spicy, it's addictive.

2 cups shredded Monterey Jack cheese (8 oz.)
1 (8-oz.) pkg. cream cheese,
   room temperature
8 oz. cottage cheese (1 cup), drained
1 teaspoon Worcestershire sauce

1 teaspoon minced green onion
1 teaspoon seasoned salt
1 (10-oz.) jar jalapeño jelly
Assorted crackers

Brush inside of a 5-1/2-cup ring mold with vegetable oil; set aside. In a food processor fitted with a metal blade, combine cheeses, Worcestershire sauce, green onion and seasoned salt. Process until blended. Firmly pack into prepared ring mold. *Complete now or make ahead.*

To complete now, cover with foil or plastic wrap; refrigerate at least 4 hours. To serve, loosen sides of cheese mixture from mold with a small metal spatula. Invert onto a platter or tray; remove mold. Spoon jelly into a small bowl; place in center of molded cheese mixture. Arrange crackers around outside of mold. To serve, let guests spread crackers with cheese mixture, then top each cracker with about 1/4 teaspoon jalapeño jelly.

To make ahead, cover with foil or plastic wrap; refrigerate spread up to 24 hours. Serve as directed above. Makes about 4 cups.

●●●

Turkey-Avocado Mousse

Fresh vegetables will disappear like magic when served with this enticing mousse.

1 (1/4-oz.) envelope unflavored gelatin
   (1 tablespoon)
1/2 cup cold water
1/2 cup dairy sour cream
1/2 cup mayonnaise
1 teaspoon seasoned salt
1/4 teaspoon pepper

1/2 teaspoon dried marjoram leaves
1 cup chopped cooked turkey or chicken
1 avocado, chopped
2 green onions, chopped
2 bacon slices, cooked, drained
1/4 cup dry white wine
Assorted fresh vegetables or crackers

In a small saucepan, combine gelatin and water; let stand 3 minutes. Stir over low heat until gelatin dissolves; set aside to cool. In a medium bowl, combine sour cream, mayonnaise, seasoned salt, pepper and marjoram; set aside. In a blender or food processor fitted with a metal blade, combine turkey or chicken, avocado, green onions, bacon and wine. Process until finely chopped but not pureed. Spoon chopped mixture into a medium bowl. Gradually stir in dissolved gelatin. Fold gelatin mixture into sour-cream mixture. Pour into an ungreased 4-cup mold. *Complete now or make ahead.*

To complete now, cover mousse with foil or plastic wrap; refrigerate at least 4 hours. Meanwhile, cut fresh vegetables into bite-sized pieces. Invert mousse onto a large platter or serving plate; remove pan. Surround mousse with vegetable pieces or crackers for spreading.

To make ahead, cover mousse with foil or plastic wrap; refrigerate up to 24 hours. Cut fresh vegetables into bite-sized pieces. Place cut vegetables in a plastic bag; seal. Refrigerate overnight. Serve as directed above. Makes about 3 cups or 12 to 15 buffet servings.

How to Make Appetizer Cheesecake

1/Spread cheese mixture evenly in an ungreased 8-inch springform pan.

2/Garnish with olives, green onions, pimento and watercress. Serve with crackers.

Appetizer Cheesecake

Memorable show-off to star at your next party.

3 cups finely shredded sharp Cheddar cheese (12 oz.)
16 oz. cottage cheese (2 cups), drained
2 tablespoons prepared horseradish
1/2 cup mayonnaise
2 tablespoons Dijon-style mustard
6 bacon slices, cooked, drained, crumbled
1 tablespoon minced fresh chives

1/4 teaspoon salt
1/8 teaspoon pepper
1/4 cup butter, melted
Sliced pitted ripe olives
Pimento strips
Sliced green onions or radishes
Watercress
Assorted crackers

In a large bowl or a food processor fitted with a metal blade, combine Cheddar cheese, cottage cheese, horseradish, mayonnaise, mustard, bacon, chives, salt, pepper and butter. Beat with electric mixer or process until blended but not smooth. Press into an ungreased 8-inch springform pan. *Complete now or make ahead.*

To complete now, cover with foil or plastic wrap; refrigerate at least 4 hours. Remove cover and side of pan. Garnish top with alternate rings of olives, pimento, green onions or radishes and watercress. Cut into thin slices or wedges; serve with crackers.

To make ahead, cover with foil or plastic wrap; refrigerate up to 24 hours. Garnish and serve as directed above. Makes 35 to 40 appetizer servings.

Salmon Spectacular

Photo on pages 10-11.

A real showpiece for your buffet spread.

2-1/2 qts. water
1 cup dry white wine
1 onion, sliced
1 celery stalk with leaves, chopped

2 bay leaves
1 teaspoon salt
1 (2-1/2- to 4-lb.) dressed whole salmon

Garnishes:
3 green onions
2 or 3 carrots

1/2 unpeeled cucumber

Fresh-Herb Topping:
1-1/2 teaspoons unflavored gelatin powder
2 tablespoons chicken broth or bouillon
1/2 cup mayonnaise
1/4 cup dairy sour cream
1/4 cup watercress leaves

1/4 cup coarsely chopped fresh parsley
3 tablespoons coarsely chopped fresh dill
1 tablespoon chopped green onion
1/4 teaspoon salt
1/8 teaspoon pepper

In a fish poacher or large roasting pan, combine water, wine, onion, celery, bay leaves and salt. Bring to boil. Measure fish at thickest part. Cut 3 layers of cheesecloth several inches longer and wider than fish. Lay salmon on center of cheesecloth. Holding cheesecloth, carefully lower salmon into simmering liquid. Cover pan; simmer 10 minutes for each inch of thickness measured or until it flakes easily when tested with a fork. Holding cheesecloth, lift salmon from pan. Place on a large platter or jelly-roll pan. *Complete now or make ahead.*

To complete now, refrigerate salmon 2 hours or until completely chilled. Meanwhile, prepare Garnishes and Fresh-Herb Topping. Remove cheesecloth; remove fins, skin and vein of dark meat from poached salmon. Place skinned fish on a large platter or tray. If gelatin mixture is syrupy and almost holds its shape, immediately spoon over top of skinned salmon. Spread mixture to cover salmon completely. If gelatin mixture is not thickened, cool in refrigerator until syrupy, checking consistency every few minutes. If necessary, spoon a thin coat of topping over salmon. Refrigerate until set; repeat with another layer of topping until all is used. While topping is still tacky, make a flower design on top of fish with reserved green-onion tops as stems and leaves, and diagonal carrot slices as flower petals. Tie onion stems with a carrot strip, if desired. Arrange cucumber slices in a fan shape at tail. Arrange long thin carrot slices on platter on both sides of salmon; decorate head area with onion brushes, if desired. Serve cold.

To make Garnishes, using 3 green tops from 1 green onion, cut 1 (6 inches) long, 1 (8 inches) long and 1 (10 inches) long, to be used as stalks for flower decoration. With scissors, cut out 6 leaf shapes from remaining green tops of same onion. Make onion brushes from remaining 2 onions by cutting stems into 2-inch lengths. Cut each onion piece lengthwise to within 1/2 inch of end. Peel carrots; cut 10 thin diagonal slices for flower petals. Using a vegetable peeler, cut remaining carrots into *very thin* lengthwise slices. Place all onions and carrots in iced water while preparing topping. Cut cucumber into thin slices.

To make Fresh-Herb Topping, in a small saucepan, combine gelatin and broth or bouillon; let stand 3 minutes. Stir over low heat until gelatin dissolves; set aside to cool. In a blender or food processor fitted with a metal blade, combine mayonnaise, sour cream, watercress, parsley, dill, green onion, salt and pepper. Process until mixture is light green with dark-green flecks. Add dissolved gelatin; process with quick on/off motions until blended.

To make ahead, refrigerate salmon up to 24 hours. Prepare Garnishes; cover and refrigerate up to 24 hours. About 2 hours before serving, prepare Fresh-Herb Topping. Add topping and garnishes as directed above. Serve cold. Makes about 15 servings.

Chocolate-Hazelnut Chiffon Cake

Scrumptious cake to serve with pride.

3 oz. semisweet chocolate
3/4 cup whole hazelnuts
2 cups all-purpose flour
1-1/2 cups sugar
1 tablespoon baking powder
1/2 teaspoon salt

1/2 cup vegetable oil
7 eggs, separated
3/4 cup cold water
1 teaspoon vanilla extract
1/2 teaspoon cream of tartar

Chocolate Glaze:
3 oz. semisweet chocolate, chopped
1 teaspoon vegetable oil

2 tablespoons butter

Melt chocolate over hot water or in a microwave; set aside. Preheat oven to 400F (205C). Spread hazelnuts in a single layer in a pie pan; bake in preheated oven 5 to 8 minutes or until skins crack. Reduce oven temperature to 325F (165C). Pour hot nuts onto center of a clean dish towel; fold towel over nuts. Rub hot nuts briskly to remove most of skins. Discard skins. Reserve 1/4 cup skinned nuts for garnish. Pour remaining skinned nuts into a blender or food processor fitted with a metal blade. With quick on/off motions, process until nuts are finely chopped but not to the consistency of peanut butter; set aside. To make cake, in a large bowl, combine flour, sugar, baking powder and salt. Make a well in center of dry mixture; add oil, egg yolks, water, vanilla and melted chocolate. Beat until smooth. Stir in chopped hazelnuts; set aside. In another large bowl, beat egg whites and cream of tartar until stiff but not dry. Gradually pour egg-yolk mixture over beaten egg whites, gently folding in while pouring. Fold in until no streaks of white remain. Spoon into an ungreased 10-inch tube pan. Bake in preheated oven 70 to 75 minutes or until a wooden pick inserted off center comes out clean. Invert pan onto a wire rack. Let stand until completely cool. Using a metal spatula, separate cake from pan; remove pan. *Complete now or make ahead.*

To complete now, prepare Chocolate Glaze. Spoon glaze over top of cake, letting some of glaze drip down sides. Garnish with reserved whole hazelnuts. Place glazed cake on a platter or serving plate. Slice to serve.

To make Chocolate Glaze, in a small saucepan, combine chocolate, oil and butter. Stir over low heat until chocolate is melted and smooth.

To make ahead, wrap cake airtight in freezer wrap; freeze up to 1 month. Thaw in wrapping at room temperature. Unwrap thawed cake; place cake on a wire rack placed over waxed paper. Glaze, decorate and serve as directed above. Makes 1 (10-inch) cake.

Note: If hazelnuts are very hard, grind in a nut grinder. Or, place skinned nuts in a plastic bag. Pound with side of a meat mallet to crack them before processing in a blender or food processor.

Emerald-Isle Shenanigan

Leprechaun Soup
Touch-of-Class Stuffed Cabbage
Spicy Brown Mustard
Killarney Potato Balls
Calico Rolls with Shamrock Garnish
Emerald-Isle Sorbet
Irish Coffee

After a long dull winter, Saint Patrick's Day is a good excuse to kick up your heels and celebrate the wearing of the green. Dress up your table with something green—place mats, candles, napkins or a shamrock—as part of a floral centerpiece. Get dinner off to a good start with bowls of piping hot Leprechaun Soup, topped with thinly sliced green onions. The star of your dinner is Touch-of-Class Stuffed Cabbage. The cabbage leaves are layered and stuffed with a delicious corned-beef mixture, then put back together to form a whole cabbage head. Homemade Spicy Brown Mustard is just the right accent, and Killarney Potato Balls complement the flavors. Serve with scrumptious, colorful Calico Rolls. For a grand finale, top off your dinner with light and refreshing Emerald-Isle Sorbet and a cup of Irish Coffee. Serves 6 people.

MAKE-AHEAD PLAN:

- **Spicy Brown Mustard**—Make up to 7 days ahead.
- **Emerald-Isle Sorbet**—Make 3 to 4 days ahead. Allow 3 to 4 hours to freeze, beat and freeze again.
- **Touch-of-Class Stuffed Cabbage**—Put together up to 24 hours ahead. Steam 1 hour before serving.
- **Calico Rolls**—Make up to 24 hours ahead. Broil immediately before serving.
- **Leprechaun Soup**—Make up to 24 hours ahead. Heat immediately before serving.
- **Killarney Potato Balls**—Cook potatoes and shape potato balls up to 24 hours ahead. Bake 15 to 20 minutes before serving.
- **Irish Coffee**—Make strong coffee just before guests arrive. Serve after dinner.

Short-Cuts:

- Purchase spicy mustard instead of making it.
- Serve commercial sherbet or sorbet instead of Emerald-Isle Sorbet.
- Use instant potatoes for Killarney Potato Balls.
- Serve regular coffee instead of Irish Coffee.

Leprechaun Soup

Hearty, yet elegant.

2 tablespoons butter or margarine
1/4 cup chopped green onions
2 medium potatoes, peeled, diced
5 cups chicken broth or bouillon
1/2 lb. Chinese pea pods
1/2 pint dairy sour cream (1 cup)
1 (8-oz.) can whole water chestnuts,
   drained, sliced

1/2 teaspoon salt
1/8 teaspoon pepper
1/4 teaspoon ground ginger
1/8 teaspoon dry mustard
Sliced green onions

In a 2-quart saucepan, melt butter or margarine. Add chopped green onions; sauté until soft. Add potatoes and broth or bouillon. Cover; simmer 20 minutes or until potatoes are tender enough to be mashed. Remove from heat; whisk briefly to partially mash potatoes. Remove stems from pea pods; cut each pod into 4 or 5 pieces; set aside. Stir 2 tablespoons hot potato mixture into sour cream. Stir sour-cream mixture into remaining potato mixture. Stir in pea-pod pieces, water chestnuts, salt, pepper, ginger and dry mustard. Over medium heat, bring to boiling point. Pour 1/2 of hot potato mixture into a blender or food processor fitted with a metal blade. Process until pureed; repeat with remaining potato mixture. *Complete now or make ahead.*

To complete now, return pureed mixture to saucepan; heat to desired temperature. Pour into individual bowls or serve in a soup tureen. Garnish with sliced green onions.

To make ahead, pour soup into a container with a tight-fitting lid; refrigerate up to 24 hours. Reheat and serve as directed above. Makes 6 servings.

Killarney Potato Balls   *Photo on pages 18-19.*

Puffy little potato balls that dress up a platter of meat.

6 medium boiling potatoes
2 tablespoons butter or margarine
1/4 cup dairy sour cream
1/2 teaspoon salt
1/8 teaspoon pepper
1 egg

1 tablespoon minced green onion
1 tablespoon minced fresh parsley
2 tablespoons butter or margarine, melted
1/4 cup grated Parmesan cheese
Parsley sprigs

Peel potatoes; cook in boiling water until tender. Drain; mash until smooth. Beat in 2 tablespoons butter or margarine, sour cream, salt, pepper, egg, green onion and parsley. Shape into 12 balls about 2 inches in diameter. *Complete now or make ahead.*

To complete now, refrigerate at least 2 hours. Preheat oven to 375F (190C). Place potato balls in an ungreased 13″ x 9″ baking pan. Brush with melted butter or margarine; sprinkle with Parmesan cheese. Bake in preheated oven 15 to 20 minutes or until lightly browned. Spoon into a medium serving bowl or serve on a platter or serving plate; serve hot.

To make ahead, refrigerate up to 24 hours. Bake and serve as directed above. Makes 6 servings.

Emerald-Isle Shenanigan

An exciting updated version of traditional corned beef and cabbage, a dish that is associated with St. Patrick's Day. Brighten the platter with a flower-like design of pimento strips plus a ring of Killarney Potato Balls.

Small green-pepper shamrocks atop the Calico Rolls accent the party theme.

Clockwise from top right: Irish Coffee, page 20, Killarney Potato Balls, page 17, Touch-of-Class Stuffed Cabbage, page 20, and Calico Rolls, page 22.

Touch-of-Class Stuffed Cabbage   *Photo on pages 18-19.*

Unusual presentation guarantees this to be a memorable dish.

4 to 5 lbs. lean corned beef, cooked,
   fat removed, cubed (2 lbs. cooked)
1 onion, quartered
1 celery stalk, cut in 1-inch pieces
1/4 cup coarsely chopped dill pickle
1/4 cup butter or margarine
1/4 cup all-purpose flour
1 cup beef broth or bouillon

1/8 teaspoon pepper
1 tablespoon Dijon-style mustard
2 eggs, separated
1/2 cup half and half
1 large head cabbage
6 thick pimento strips
1 pimento-stuffed green olive
Spicy Brown Mustard, opposite

In a food processor fitted with a metal blade, finely chop 1/2 of cooked corned beef; do not puree. Place in a large bowl. Repeat with remaining corned beef. Chop onion, celery and dill pickle separately in food processor, placing each in large bowl with chopped corned beef. In a small saucepan, melt butter or margarine. Add flour; stirring constantly, cook 2 minutes. Gradually stir in broth or bouillon, pepper and Dijon-style mustard. In a small bowl, lightly beat egg yolks; stir in half and half. Stir egg-yolk mixture into mustard mixture. Stirring constantly, cook until thickened. Stir into meat mixture. In another small bowl, beat egg whites until stiff but not dry. Fold into meat mixture; set aside. Trim and discard any undesirable outer leaves and hard core of cabbage. Carefully remove leaves from cabbage head. Drop 4 or 5 leaves at a time into boiling water; boil 2 minutes or until softened. Drain leaves; trim and discard hard center veins. Place an 18-inch square of cheesecloth in center of a large round plate. Slightly overlap 4 or 5 of largest leaves in a circle in center of cheesecloth. Spoon about 1/2 cup meat mixture onto center of leaves. Use a small spatula to spread meat mixture over leaves. Place 4 or 5 of next largest leaves on filling; cover with another layer of meat mixture. Continue layering with progressively smaller leaves, using less meat mixture for each layer until all leaves and filling are used. Carefully pull up cheesecloth around filled cabbage leaves to reconstruct shape of cabbage head. Twist edges of cheesecloth together; tie with string. *Complete now or make ahead.*

To complete now, pour hot water 1 inch deep in a 6- or 8-quart pan. Place cheesecloth-wrapped cabbage on a steamer rack; place in pan over hot water. Cover pan; steam 60 minutes, adding more hot water, if needed. With a large fork, lift cabbage from pan; remove and discard cheesecloth. Place steamed cabbage on a platter. Garnish with pimento strips and green olive; cut into wedges. Serve hot with Spicy Brown Mustard.

To make ahead, cover stuffed cabbage and cheesecloth with foil. Refrigerate up to 24 hours. Steam and serve as directed above. Makes 6 to 8 servings.

•••

Irish Coffee   *Photo on pages 18-19.*

Traditional way to top off a St. Patrick's Day dinner.

2 tablespoons sugar
5 cups hot very strong coffee

1/2 cup Irish whiskey
Whipped Cream

Spoon about 1 teaspoon sugar into each of 6 Irish-coffee glasses or regular coffee cups. Pour about 1 tablespoon hot coffee into each glass or cup. Stir until sugar dissolves. Add hot coffee to each glass or cup until at least 3/4 full. Add about 1-1/2 tablespoons whiskey to each. Top each with a dollop of whipped cream. Serve hot. Makes 6 servings.

How to Make Touch-of-Class Stuffed Cabbage

1/Over cheesecloth, begin layering blanched cabbage leaves and meat mixture.

2/Carefully pull up cheesecloth around leaves to reconstruct cabbage shape.

Spicy Brown Mustard

Adds punch to corned beef.

2 tablespoons mustard seeds
1/4 cup red-wine vinegar
1/4 cup dry red wine
2 tablespoons dry mustard
1/4 cup water

1 teaspoon prepared horseradish
1/8 teaspoon ground turmeric
1/8 teaspoon ground cloves
1 tablespoon brown sugar

In a blender, combine mustard seeds and vinegar. Process until seeds are partially crushed and form a paste. Let stand 5 minutes. Pour wine into a 1-quart saucepan. Stir in dry mustard, water, horseradish, turmeric, cloves, brown sugar and vinegar mixture. Stirring constantly, cook over low heat 6 to 8 minutes or until thickened. Set aside to cool. *Complete now or make ahead.*

To complete now, spoon cooled mixture into a small serving dish. Cover with foil or plastic wrap; let stand at least 2 hours to let flavors blend.

To make ahead, spoon into a container with a tight-fitting lid. Refrigerate up to 7 days. Serve as directed above. Makes about 2/3 cup.

Calico Rolls

Photo on pages 18-19.

Colorful open-faced rolls.

3 (6-inch) French rolls
3/4 cup shredded Cheddar cheese (3 oz.)
3 tablespoons butter or margarine,
   room temperature

1/3 cup chopped pitted ripe olives
1/4 cup chopped green bell pepper
2 tablespoons chopped pimento

Shamrock Garnishes:
2 large green bell peppers

Split rolls in half lengthwise. In a medium bowl, combine cheese, butter or margarine, olives, bell pepper and pimento. Spread cheese mixture on cut sides of rolls. Place cut-side up in an ungreased shallow baking pan. *Complete now or make ahead.*

To complete now, prepare Shamrock Garnishes; preheat broiler. Broil rolls about 5 inches from heat until cheese melts. Top each broiled roll with a shamrock garnish; arrange garnished rolls on a platter or serving plate. Serve warm.

To make Shamrock Garnishes, draw or trace a 1-1/2- to 2-inch shamrock design from a St. Patrick's paper napkin or decoration. Using pattern, cut 6 shamrock designs from green peppers. Store shamrocks in a small plastic bag in refrigerator until served.

To make ahead, cover filled rolls with foil or plastic wrap; refrigerate up to 24 hours. Broil, garnish and serve as directed above. Makes 6 servings.

— • ● • —

Emerald-Isle Sorbet

As refreshing as an Irish spring.

1 cup water
3/4 cup sugar
1/4 cup light corn syrup

2 cups grapefruit juice
1/4 cup green crème de menthe liqueur
3 or 4 drops green food coloring, if desired

In a medium saucepan, combine water, sugar and corn syrup. Stirring constantly, cook until sugar dissolves. Remove from heat; add grapefruit juice, crème de menthe and food coloring, if desired. Pour into a 9" x 5" loaf pan; cover with foil or plastic wrap. *Complete now or make ahead.*

To complete now, place in freezer until almost firm, 1 to 3 hours. Break frozen mixture into small pieces. In a chilled bowl, blender or food processor fitted with a metal blade, beat or process until smooth and fluffy but not thawed. Return beaten mixture to pan; freeze until firm, 1 to 3 hours. For a smoother texture, beat mixture a second time; freeze until served. Spoon or scoop into balls. Serve in individual dessert dishes.

To make ahead, freeze up to 4 days. Break frozen mixture into small pieces. In a chilled bowl, blender or food processor fitted with a metal blade, beat or process once or twice as directed above. Serve as directed above. Makes about 1 quart.

Celebrating Easter

Cheese & Sausage Squares
Pork Loin with Fresh Herbs
Roasted New Potatoes
Carrots Siam
Spiced Zucchini Sticks
Jalapeño Spirals
Double-Almond Easter Cake

Nations around the world celebrate Easter with traditional foods that vary as much as the countries where they originate. In some countries, Easter dinner is the culmination of many weeks of planning and cooking. But the meal can be simplified. With make-ahead planning, everyone can join in the celebration.

Pork Loin with Fresh Herbs is coated with fresh herbs the night before so it has a divine aroma and flavor on Easter. While it roasts, you'll have time to watch the children hunt for eggs. Spiced Zucchini Sticks, prepared days ahead of time, contribute a pleasant spicy sweet-sour flavor to the meal. Jalapeño Spirals add a slightly nippy flavor.

Following the theme of the day, Double-Almond Easter Cake is just right after this special dinner. Pastel-colored almonds resemble miniature Easter eggs on the cake. Serves 8 people.

MAKE-AHEAD PLAN:

- **Cheese & Sausage Squares**—Make and freeze up to 3 weeks ahead. Thaw frozen squares in refrigerator overnight. Or, bake and refrigerate up to 24 hours. Heat just before dinner.
- **Spiced Zucchini Sticks**—Make up to 7 days ahead.
- **Double-Almond Easter Cake**—Make up to 24 hours ahead; cover and store at room temperature.
- **Jalapeño Spirals**—Refrigerate shaped rolls up to 24 hours. About 1-1/2 hours before serving, remove spirals from refrigerator. Let stand covered at room temperature until almost doubled in bulk before baking.
- **Pork Loin with Fresh Herbs**—Cover roast with herbs up to 24 hours ahead.
- **Carrots Siam**—Steam or cook up to 12 hours ahead or early on Easter morning. Heat with seasonings at serving time.
- **Roasted New Potatoes**—Roast on Easter morning with pork loin.

Short-Cuts:

- Cook and serve commercially frozen buttered carrots.
- Steam zucchini; omit spices.
- Purchase similar cake at bakery.

Jalapeño Spirals

Filling is creamy and spicy but not hot.

1 (1/4-oz.) pkg. active dry yeast (1 tablespoon)	1/2 teaspoon salt
1/4 cup warm water (110F, 45C)	1 egg
1/4 cup warm milk (110F, 45C)	1-1/2 to 2 cups all-purpose flour
2 tablespoons sugar	2 (3-oz.) pkgs. cream cheese, room temperature
3 tablespoons butter or margarine, room temperature	1/4 cup jalapeño jelly

In a medium bowl, soften yeast in water. Stir in milk, sugar, butter or margarine, salt, egg and 1 cup flour. Beat until smooth. Stir in enough remaining flour to make a soft dough. Turn out onto a lightly floured surface; knead until smooth and elastic. Clean and grease bowl. Place dough in bowl, turning to grease all sides. Cover; let rise in a warm place until doubled in bulk. Grease a round 9-inch cake pan. Punch down dough. On a lightly floured surface, roll out to a 15" x 9" rectangle. Spread with cream cheese to 1 inch from edge; then spread with jalapeño jelly. Starting on a long edge, roll up dough, jelly-roll style. Pinch seam to seal; cut roll into 10 equal slices. Arrange slices, cut-side down, in greased pan. *Complete now or make ahead.*

To complete now, cover; let rise in a warm place until doubled in bulk. Preheat oven to 375F (190C). Bake in preheated oven 25 minutes or until lightly browned. Serve warm on a platter.

To make ahead, cover pan with foil or plastic wrap; refrigerate up to 24 hours. About 1-1/2 hours before serving, remove spirals from refrigerator. Let stand covered at room temperature about 1 hour or until almost doubled in bulk. Bake and serve as directed above. Makes 10 rolls.

Pork Loin with Fresh Herbs

Pork flavor is enhanced by fresh herbs and kept moist with apple cider.

1 (5-1/2- to 6-lb.) pork-loin center-rib roast, backbone removed	1 tablespoon coarsely chopped fresh marjoram leaves or 1/4 teaspoon dried leaf marjoram
1/2 teaspoon salt	1/4 cup coarsely chopped celery leaves
1/4 teaspoon pepper	1/2 cup apple cider or apple juice
1/4 cup coarsely chopped fresh sage or 1 teaspoon dried sage	

Cut a 24" x 18" piece of heavy foil. Place roast, fat-side up, in center of foil. Sprinkle roast with salt and pepper. Combine sage, marjoram and celery leaves; pat herbs over fat. Carefully fold foil over roast; crimp or fold edges together. *Complete now or make ahead.*

To complete now, place wrapped roast in a roasting pan or large shallow baking pan; place pan in oven. Turn oven to 325F (165C). Roast 1 hour. Open foil; tuck around base of roast. Carefully spoon apple cider or apple juice over roast. Continue roasting 1-1/2 to 2 hours longer or until a meat thermometer inserted in center of roast registers 170F (75C). To serve, cut between ribs. Spoon meat drippings over each serving. Serve hot.

To make ahead, refrigerate foil-wrapped roast up to 24 hours. Roast and serve as directed above. Makes 8 or 9 servings.

How to Make Jalapeño Spirals

1/Spread jalapeño jelly over cream cheese to 1 inch from edge. Roll up dough jelly-roll style.

2/Arrange rolls, cut-side down, in pan. Refrigerate up to 24 hours, or let rise at room temperature.

Cheese & Sausage Squares

Delightful melt-in-your-mouth morsels.

1/2 lb. hot and spicy, bulk pork sausage, crumbled
3 eggs, lightly beaten
16 oz. cottage cheese (2 cups)
1 tablespoon minced fresh chives

1/4 teaspoon salt
5 filo-dough sheets
1/2 cup butter, melted
2 tablespoons grated Parmesan cheese

In a small skillet, brown sausage; drain thoroughly. In a medium bowl, combine eggs, cottage cheese, chives, salt and drained cooked sausage; set aside. Preheat oven to 400F (205C). Keep filo sheets covered to prevent drying. Brush 3 filo sheets with some of butter; stack sheets, buttered-sides up. Fold stacked buttered sheets in half crosswise. Place folded layers in a 12" x 7-1/2" baking dish. Carefully spread sausage mixture over folded filo. Sprinkle with Parmesan cheese. Brush butter over remaining 2 filo sheets; stack, buttered-sides up. Fold in half crosswise; lightly press 2 folded filo sheets over sausage mixture. Brush top with butter. Bake in preheated oven 25 to 30 minutes or until top is browned. *Complete now or make ahead.*

To complete now, let stand 10 minutes. Cut into squares; serve hot.

To make ahead, cool completely. Cover with foil or freezer wrap; refrigerate overnight, or freeze up to 3 weeks. Thaw frozen loaf in refrigerator overnight. To reheat, remove cover; place in a cold oven. Turn oven to 375F (190C). Heat 10 to 15 minutes or until loaf is heated through. Cut and serve as directed above. Makes 24 appetizer squares.

How to Make Double-Almond Easter Cake

1/Add flour alternately with sour cream; beat with an electric mixer until smooth.

2/Before glaze sets, arrange 5 clusters of 5 almonds each on top to resemble spring flowers.

Spiced Zucchini Sticks

They look like cucumbers, but are actually zucchini.

2 tablespoons salt
3 medium zucchini, each cut lengthwise
   into 8 strips
1 onion, sliced
1-1/2 cups cider vinegar

3/4 cup sugar
1/4 teaspoon ground turmeric
1/2 teaspoon celery seeds
1/2 teaspoon whole mixed pickling spices

In a large bowl, stir salt into 1 quart water until dissolved. Add zucchini and onion. Cover with plastic wrap; let stand at least 2 hours. Drain thoroughly. In a 2-quart pan, combine vinegar, sugar, turmeric, celery seeds and pickling spices. Bring to a boil; add drained zucchini and onion. Simmer 2 to 3 minutes or until zucchini is tender but not soft. Let cool in liquid. *Complete now or make ahead.*

To complete now, drain; serve zucchini strips and onions in a serving bowl.

To make ahead, transfer cooked zucchini and liquid to a container with a tight-fitting lid; refrigerate up to 7 days. Drain and serve as directed above. Makes about 3 cups.

Double-Almond Easter Cake

Almond paste plus almond liqueur provide a double flavor reward.

3/4 cup butter or margarine,
  room temperature
1 (7-oz.) pkg. almond paste, crumbled
1-1/2 cups sugar
6 eggs

1/4 teaspoon salt
1/2 teaspoon baking soda
3 cups all-purpose flour
1/2 cup dairy sour cream
2 tablespoons almond-flavored liqueur

Glaze:
1-1/2 cups sifted powdered sugar
1 tablespoon almond-flavored liqueur
1 tablespoon lemon juice

1 tablespoon butter, melted
2 to 3 tablespoons milk
25 pastel-colored candy-coated almonds

Preheat oven to 325F (165C). Grease and flour a 10-inch tube pan; set aside. In a large bowl, use an electric mixer to beat butter or margarine and almond paste until smooth. Add sugar; beat until fluffy. Beat in eggs, 1 at a time, beating well after each addition. Beat in salt and baking soda. Stir in flour alternately with sour cream; beat with electric mixer until smooth. Stir in liqueur. Spoon into prepared pan. Bake in preheated oven about 70 minutes or until a wooden pick inserted in center comes out clean. Let stand in pan on a wire rack 15 minutes. Loosen cake from pan with a metal spatula. Invert onto a cooling rack; remove pan. Let cool completely. Prepare glaze. Lightly spread glaze on top and side of cake. Before glaze sets, arrange 5 clusters of 5 almonds each on top to resemble spring flowers. *Complete now or make ahead.*

To make Glaze, in a small bowl, combine powdered sugar, liqueur, lemon juice and butter. If mixture is too thick for a glaze, add milk a few drops at a time.

To complete now, after glaze sets, cut into wedges to serve.

To make ahead, lightly cover decorated cake with plastic wrap. Store at room temperature up to 24 hours. To serve, cut in wedges. Makes 1 (10-inch) cake.

●●●

Carrots Siam

An everyday vegetable that's lifted out of the doldrums with an easy sauce.

6 large carrots or
  1 (16-oz.) pkg. frozen baby carrots
2 tablespoons butter or margarine

2 tablespoons fruit chutney, finely chopped
1/4 teaspoon ground ginger

Peel fresh carrots; cut into julienne pieces. Steam or cook carrot pieces or frozen carrots in lightly salted water 3 to 4 minutes or until tender; drain. *Complete now or make ahead.*

To complete now, in a medium skillet, melt butter or margarine. Stir in chutney and ginger. Add cooked carrots. Stirring frequently, cook over medium-low heat until hot and glazed. Spoon into a medium serving bowl; serve hot.

To make ahead, cool cooked carrots under cold running water to prevent overcooking; place in a plastic bag. Seal and refrigerate up to 12 hours. Glaze cooked carrots as directed above; serve hot. Makes 6 to 8 servings.

Mom's Brunch Treat

Mom's Eye Opener
French-Toast Supreme
Warm Maple Syrup
Homemade Pork & Potato Sausage
Fresh Strawberry Treat
Suisse-Mocha Coffee

*I*t's Mother's Day! Time to turn the tables and let Mom be the special guest of honor for a family brunch. Children from kindergarten up can contribute to this event. Assign chores according to age, with the younger children setting the table or washing and arranging strawberries. Let teenagers or Dad take charge of the make-ahead main dishes. The featured dish, French-Toast Supreme, is easy to put together the day before. Refrigerate it overnight. When baked the next day, it's beautifully golden and practically melts in your mouth. Homemade Pork & Potato Sausage is worthy of being served on a special day. If it is too involved for your group to manage, make patties from prepared bulk pork sausage.

Now to the fun part! Purchase two pints of the largest and most beautiful strawberries with stems you can find. Arrange them on the prettiest tray in the house. Fill one small bowl with dairy sour cream and another with brown sugar. After everyone finishes the main part of the meal, clear the table and surprise Mom with this spectacular tray. Let everyone dip their strawberries in sour cream, then in brown sugar. Guaranteed to be a hit! Serves about 6 people.

MAKE-AHEAD PLAN:

- **Mom's Eye-Opener**—Make basic mixture up to 2 days ahead. Add tomato juice before serving.
- **Homemade Pork & Potato Sausage**—Make up to 24 hours ahead. Fry until partially cooked. Finish cooking just before serving.
- **French-Toast Supreme**—Make up to 24 hours ahead.
- **Maple Syrup**—Heat just before serving.
- **Fresh Strawberry Treat**—Purchase strawberries no more than 24 hours ahead. Refrigerate strawberries in a rigid plastic container with a tight-fitting lid or in a plastic bag, removing as much air from bag as possible.
- **Suisse-Mocha Coffee**—Boil water while arranging strawberries on tray. Make 1 cup of flavored coffee for each adult by following directions on container. Another flavored instant coffee may be used.

Short-Cuts:

- Buy links or bulk pork sausage instead of making Homemade Pork & Potato Sausage.
- Make regular French toast instead of French-Toast Supreme.

French-Toast Supreme

Make it the day before to let the flavors mingle.

1/2 (16-oz.) loaf French bread or
   1 (8-oz.) baguette
4 eggs
1/3 cup orange juice
1/2 teaspoon grated orange peel
1-1/4 cups milk

2 tablespoons butter or margarine, melted
1/8 teaspoon ground cinnamon
2 tablespoons brown sugar
Maple syrup or honey, if desired
Mandarin-orange sections

Cut bread in half horizontally. Starting at cut surfaces, cut in 1-inch slices, almost to bottom crust. Leave a small amount of crust at bottom uncut to hold it together. Place both halves, cut-side up, in an ungreased 13" x 9" baking dish; set aside. In a small bowl, beat eggs; stir in orange juice, orange peel, milk and butter or margarine. Spoon over cut surfaces of bread. Let stand 5 minutes. Using a pancake turner, carefully turn basted bread cut-side down. In a small bowl, combine cinnamon and brown sugar. Sprinkle cinnamon mixture over coated bread; cover with foil or plastic wrap. *Complete now or make ahead.*

To complete now, refrigerate at least 2 hours. Preheat oven to 325F (165C). Remove cover from dish. Bake in preheated oven 30 to 40 minutes or until golden brown and firm. To serve, cut slices apart; arrange on a platter or serving plate. Serve with maple syrup or honey, if desired. Garnish with orange sections; serve hot.

To make ahead, refrigerate up to 24 hours. Remove cover from dish; bake, serve and garnish as directed above. Makes 6 servings.

●●●

Mom's Eye-Opener

Make the basic mixture ahead and stir in the tomato juice at the last minute.

1/2 cup chopped celery
2 tablespoons chopped onion
2 tablespoons chopped parsley
2 (10-1/2-oz.) cans condensed beef broth

1/4 teaspoon salt
1/8 teaspoon seasoned pepper
1 qt. tomato juice (4 cups)
Celery stalks

In a medium saucepan, combine celery, onion, parsley, undiluted beef broth, salt and seasoned pepper. Bring to a boil; reduce heat. Simmer 10 minutes. Puree in blender or food processor fitted with a metal blade. Line a sieve with 2 thicknesses of cheesecloth. Pour puree through lined sieve into a 1/2-gallon pitcher. Discard vegetables. Stir tomato juice into puree. *Complete now or make ahead.*

To complete now, pour into a large saucepan. Stir occasionally over medium heat until warmed through. Pour into mugs; serve warm with celery-stalk stirrers. To serve cold, chill in refrigerator; serve in drinking glasses.

To make ahead, cover and refrigerate up to 3 days. Serve warm or cold as directed above. Makes 6 to 7 servings.

Homemade Pork & Potato Sausage

Mellow blending of spices gives character and a delicious flavor.

1-1/4 lbs. pork shoulder or leg,	**1 teaspoon pepper**
cut in 1- to 2-inch cubes	**3/4 teaspoon ground sage**
1/4 lb. pork fat, cubed	**1/4 teaspoon dried leaf thyme**
1 medium potato, peeled, cooked, diced	**1/4 teaspoon ground nutmeg**
1 teaspoon salt	**1 tablespoon minced fresh chives**

In a food processor fitted with a metal blade, combine 1/2 of pork, 1/2 of pork fat and all of potato. Process until mixture has texture of ground meat. Remove to a large bowl. Repeat with remaining pork and fat. Stir in salt, pepper, sage, thyme, nutmeg and chives. Cover bowl with foil or plastic wrap; refrigerate at least 6 hours to let flavors blend. *Complete now or make ahead.*

To complete now, shape sausage into 2-1/2-inch patties. In a large skillet, fry until cooked through. Drain and arrange cooked sausage patties on a platter or serving plate; serve immediately.

To make ahead, shape sausage mixture into 2-1/2-inch patties. In a large skillet, lightly brown patties on both sides; do not cook completely. Place on a platter or serving plate; cover with foil or plastic wrap. Refrigerate up to 24 hours. Preheat oven to 325F (165C). Arrange partially cooked patties in a single layer in an ungreased 13″ x 9″ baking pan. Cover pan with a lid or foil; bake in preheated oven 10 to 15 minutes or until done. Drain and serve as directed above. Makes 6 servings.

Fresh Strawberry Treat   *Photo on page 28.*

You won't believe how good these are and with so little work!

2 pints jumbo strawberries with stems	**1/2 cup lightly packed brown sugar**
1/2 cup dairy sour cream	

Rinse strawberries; *do not remove stems.* Drain on paper towels until dry. *Complete now or make ahead.*

To complete now, spoon sour cream and brown sugar into separate small bowls. Use a fork to fluff brown sugar so it is no longer packed. Place bowls in center of a large decorative tray. Arrange rinsed strawberries around bowls. Serve as a dessert. Let diners dip strawberries in sour cream, then in brown sugar.

To make ahead, lightly dampen paper towels. Place a layer of damp towels in a firm plastic container with a tight-fitting lid. Arrange strawberries on damp paper towels, placing a layer of damp towels between layers of strawberries. Refrigerate up to 24 hours. Serve as directed above. Makes 6 servings.

Picnic-in-the-Park with Dad

Smoked-Salmon Butter   Crackers or Toast
Picnic-in-the-Park Steak
Smoky Baked Limas
Zucchini-Mushroom Salad
Four-Corners' Salad
Beer & Soft Drinks
Chocolate & Peanut-Butter-Swirl Cake

Everyone in the family will enjoy honoring Dad on his day with a picnic in the park. Our menu is designed so everything is done ahead except actually barbecuing the steak and heating rolls and onion topping.

Carefully plan for any special equipment to keep hot foods hot and cold foods cold. Frozen packets of artificial ice are handy supplements to ice cubes. Plastic bowls with tight-fitting lids protect salads and keep them from spilling enroute.

To keep Smoky Baked Limas hot, bake them just before you leave the house. Transport them in the baking dish or an electric slow-cooker. Wrap the container in 5 or 6 layers of newspaper.

While you're waiting for the barbecue grill to get hot, enjoy Smoked-Salmon Butter on crackers or toast with your beer or soft drinks. Serves about 6 people.

MAKE-AHEAD PLAN:

- **Chocolate & Peanut-Butter-Swirl Cake**—Make 1 to 2 days ahead.
- **Picnic-in-the-Park Steak**—Marinate up to 24 hours ahead; prepare onion sauce 2 to 3 hours before serving. Heat sauce and rolls on grill. Be sure to take briquets, matches, tongs, a pan for heating sauce, a small grill, and a board and sharp knife for cutting meat.
- **Smoky Baked Limas**—Soak, simmer and season up to 24 hours ahead. Bake before picnic.
- **Four-Corners' Salad**—Make up to 24 hours ahead.
- **Zucchini-Mushroom Salad**—Make up to 24 hours ahead. Combine just before picnic.
- **Smoked-Salmon Butter**—Make up to 24 hours ahead.

Short-Cuts:

- Purchase a cake at a bakery instead of making Chocolate & Peanut-Butter-Swirl Cake.
- Omit 1 salad.
- Barbecue plain steak, without marinade and onions.

Clockwise from top: Smoky Baked Limas, page 35, Zucchini-Mushroom Salad, page 35, Picnic-in-the-Park Steak, page 34.

Picnic-in-the-Park Steak

Photo on page 33.

Get everything ready at home for a hassle-free picnic.

1/2 cup dry red wine
1 garlic clove, crushed
1/4 cup vegetable oil
1/2 teaspoon ground ginger
2 tablespoons soy sauce
1/4 teaspoon salt
1/8 teaspoon pepper

1 (3-lb.) boneless top-sirloin steak
   (about 2 inches thick)
6 French rolls
Butter or margarine
2 onions, thinly sliced
1 cup beef broth or bouillon

In an 11″ x 7″ dish or plastic container with a tight-fitting lid, combine red wine, garlic, oil, ginger, soy sauce, salt and pepper. Add steak; spoon sauce over steak. *Complete now or make ahead.*

To complete now, cover with foil or plastic wrap; marinate steak in refrigerator at least 4 hours. Meanwhile, cut rolls in half lengthwise. Butter cut sides; wrap buttered rolls in foil. Before going to picnic, drain steak; reserve marinade. In a medium skillet, melt 2 tablespoons butter or margarine. Add onions; sauté until soft. Stir in reserved marinade and broth or bouillon; cook over medium-high heat 5 minutes. Let cool slightly; pour into a 4- or 6-cup container with a tight-fitting lid for transporting to picnic. Transport meat in an ice chest, in container used for marinating. At picnic, pour onion sauce into a small saucepan. Place on side of grill until heated through. Place foil-wrapped rolls on edge of grill during final 10 minutes steak is broiled. Broil drained steak on a hibachi or barbecue grill, about 4 inches from heat, 10 minutes on each side or until of desired doneness. Thinly slice cooked meat; place a hot open-faced roll on each plate. Place some of sliced meat on rolls; top each with some of hot onion sauce. Add tops of rolls or serve open-faced.

To make ahead, cover; refrigerate steak in marinade up to 24 hours. Prepare onion sauce up to 3 hours ahead. Transport, cook and serve as directed above. Makes 6 servings.

Smoked-Salmon Butter

Use dry-smoked salmon, not the more moist, thinly sliced lox.

1/2 lb. dry-smoked salmon
1/2 cup butter, room temperature
1 tablespoon lemon juice
1/2 teaspoon dried dill weed

1/8 teaspoon pepper
1 tablespoon minced fresh chives
2 tablespoons dairy sour cream
Crackers or Melba toast

Remove skin and bones from salmon; cut into 1-inch pieces. In a blender or food processor fitted with a metal blade, combine salmon pieces, butter, lemon juice, dill weed, pepper, chives and sour cream. Process until smooth. Spoon into a small bowl or crock with a tight-fitting lid. *Complete now or make ahead.*

To complete now, refrigerate up to 2 hours. Carry to picnic in a cooler. About 15 minutes before serving, remove from cooler. To serve, spread on crackers or Melba toast.

To make ahead, cover tightly; refrigerate up to 24 hours. Transport and serve as directed above. Makes 1-1/2 cups.

Zucchini-Mushroom Salad

Photo on page 33.

If you grow your own zucchini, you'll want to prepare this salad often.

3 tablespoons vegetable oil
1 lb. zucchini, cut in 1/4-inch slices
1/4 cup chopped onion
1 garlic clove, crushed
1/2 lb. mushrooms (about 20 medium), sliced
1/3 cup vinegar

1 tablespoon sugar
1/2 teaspoon dried dill weed
1/3 cup dairy sour cream
1/4 cup grated Parmesan cheese (3/4 oz.)
1/4 teaspoon salt
Dill sprig, if desired

In a large skillet, heat oil. Add zucchini, onion and garlic. Sauté until zucchini is crisp-tender. Add mushrooms; simmer 1 to 2 minutes; remove from heat. In a medium bowl, combine vinegar, sugar and dill weed; stir until sugar dissolves. Add sautéed vegetables; toss well to coat. *Complete now or make ahead.*

To complete now, refrigerate 3 to 4 hours to let flavors blend. Drain, reserving 2 tablespoons liquid in a small bowl. Stir in sour cream, Parmesan cheese and salt. Pour over chilled vegetable mixture. Cover airtight; transport in an ice chest. To serve, toss; garnish with dill sprig, if desired. Serve chilled.

To make ahead, refrigerate up to 24 hours. Drain; prepare sour-cream dressing. Garnish and serve as directed above. Makes 6 or 7 servings.

Smoky Baked Limas

Photo on page 33.

The best-ever lima beans.

1 lb. dry small lima beans
2 qts. water (1/2 gal.)
1 large onion, chopped
1/2 lb. smoked sausage
1/4 cup lightly packed brown sugar
2 tablespoons Dijon-style mustard
1 teaspoon Worcestershire sauce

1 garlic clove, crushed
1/4 cup molasses
1/4 cup ketchup
1/8 teaspoon ground cloves
1 teaspoon salt
1/8 teaspoon pepper

In a 4-quart saucepan, combine beans and water. Bring to boil; let boil 2 minutes. Remove from heat; cover and let stand 1 hour. Add onion. Bring bean mixture to a boil; cover. Reduce heat; simmer 1 to 1-1/4 hours or until beans are tender. Cut several slices from smoked sausage; dice remaining sausage. Drain beans, reserving liquid. In a large nonmetal casserole dish, combine diced smoked sausage, brown sugar, mustard, Worcestershire sauce, garlic, molasses, ketchup, cloves, salt and pepper. Stir in drained, cooked beans. *Complete now or make ahead.*

To complete now, place casserole in oven. Turn oven temperature to 300F (150C). Bake 1-1/2 to 2 hours, adding reserved bean liquid as needed. Garnish top with reserved sliced smoked sausage. To transport to picnic, cover baked casserole with foil or a lid. Wrap casserole with 5 or 6 layers of newspaper, if desired. Or, pour beans into a slow-cooker; cover with lid. Wrap in newspaper to transport.

To make ahead, do not bake. Cover reserved liquid and bean mixture with foil or plastic wrap. Refrigerate separately up to 24 hours. About 2 hours before serving, remove cover from bean mixture; stir. Bake beans as directed above, adding reserved bean liquid as needed. Transport as directed above. Makes 6 to 8 servings.

How to Make Four-Corners' Salad

1/Toss vegetables with cheese cubes and 1/2 of crumbled bacon.

2/Transport in a covered container. To serve, toss; top with remaining bacon.

Four-Corners' Salad

A hearty, make-ahead salad for your next picnic.

6 bacon slices
1 (15-oz.) can white hominy, well drained
1 (15-oz.) can red kidney beans,
   well drained
1/2 small red onion, sliced
1 cup chopped celery
1/4 cup sweet-pickle relish

1/2 cup cubed Cheddar cheese (2 oz.)
1/3 cup mayonnaise
2 teaspoons vinegar
2 teaspoons prepared mustard
1/2 teaspoon seasoned salt
1/8 teaspoon pepper
Celery leaves or other green leaves

Fry bacon until crisp; drain on paper towels. Crumble drained bacon; set aside. In a large bowl, combine hominy, beans, onion, celery, pickle relish, cheese and 1/2 of crumbled bacon. In a small bowl, combine mayonnaise, vinegar, mustard, seasoned salt and pepper. Add to hominy mixture; toss lightly to coat. Spoon into a container with a tight-fitting lid. *Complete now or make ahead.*

To complete now, transport to picnic in container. Toss before serving; top with remaining bacon. Garnish with celery leaves or other green leaves. Serve cold

To make ahead, refrigerate up to 24 hours. Transport and serve as directed above. Makes 6 or 7 servings.

Chocolate & Peanut-Butter-Swirl Cake

An easy-to-make cake that is specially designed for chocolate and peanut-butter addicts.

3 oz. semisweet chocolate
1-3/4 cups all-purpose flour
1 cup granulated sugar
1/2 cup lightly packed brown sugar
1-1/2 teaspoons baking soda
1/2 teaspoon salt

1-1/4 cups buttermilk
1/2 cup vegetable shortening
2 eggs
1 teaspoon vanilla extract
1/4 cup chunk-style peanut butter

Fudge Frosting:
4 oz. semisweet chocolate, chopped
1 lb. powdered sugar, sifted
1/2 cup butter or margarine, melted

1 teaspoon vanilla extract
1/4 cup milk
1/2 cup coarsely chopped peanuts

Melt chocolate over hot water or in a microwave; set aside. Grease and flour 2 round 9-inch cake pans; set aside. Preheat oven to 350F (175C). In a large bowl, combine flour, granulated sugar, brown sugar, baking soda, salt, buttermilk, shortening, eggs and vanilla. Beat with an electric mixer at low speed 1/2 minute. Increase speed to medium-high; beat 3 minutes. Pour 1-1/2 cups mixture into a small bowl; beat in peanut butter. Set peanut-butter mixture aside. Add melted chocolate to remaining mixture in large bowl. Pour 1/2 of chocolate batter into each prepared pan. With a large spoon, drop peanut-butter mixture in mounds on top of chocolate batter. Pull a narrow spatula through batter in pans in a zig-zag motion to create a marbled effect. Bake in preheated oven 30 to 35 minutes or until a wooden pick inserted in center of cake comes out clean. Cool in pans 10 minutes on a wire rack. Turn out on rack. Remove pans; cool completely. *Complete now or make ahead.*

To complete now, prepare Fudge Frosting; spread about 1/3 of frosting between cake layers. Spread remaining frosting over top and side of cake. Sprinkle with chopped peanuts. Let stand until frosting sets. Place in a cake carrier; transport to picnic in carrier.

To make Fudge Frosting, melt chocolate over hot water or in a microwave. In a medium bowl, combine powdered sugar, butter or margarine, vanilla, milk and melted chocolate. Beat until smooth.

To make ahead, wrap cake layers airtight in freezer wrap or heavy foil. Store in freezer up to 2 weeks. Thaw cake layers at room temperature. Or, make and frost cake 1 or 2 days ahead. Store at room temperature in a cake carrier; transport in carrier. Makes 1 (9-inch) 2-layer cake.

Trick-or-Treat Party

Goblin's Drumsticks
Banana-Orange-Yogurt Cups
Peanut-Butter & Jam Jack-O'-Lanterns
Bewitching Gorp
Orange Juice or Orange Drink

An alternative to youngsters going *trick or treating* along dark streets, is to have a special Halloween party for them. Round up their friends and plan activities suitable for their age group.

As the young goblins arrive, present each with a *treat box* filled with goodies. Instead of candy, this box actually contains a finger-food supper. There's a Goblin's Drumstick, which is a crunchy, ready-to-eat chicken drumstick. Banana-Orange-Yogurt Cup—a gelatin mixture—and a smiling Peanut-Butter & Jam Jack-O'-Lantern cookie will both be winners with the youngsters. To top it off, there's Bewitching Gorp and an individual carton of orange juice or orange drink.

To dress up the treat boxes, have friends and neighbors help you save children's shoe boxes or other suitable boxes. Cover each box with orange-colored paper or wrapping paper with a Halloween design. Use five- or six-ounce paper cups with lids for molding each gelatin serving. Party shops or fast-food stores should have what you need.

Foods in our menu will fill 10 or 12 treat boxes. If you have as many as 12 guests, make the gelatin servings slightly smaller. There are extra Peanut-Butter & Jam Jack-O'-Lanterns for you to give other trick or treaters who ring your doorbell. No more than 30 minutes before guests arrive, place food in the treat boxes. Refrigerate until guests arrive. Serves 10 to 12 people.

MAKE-AHEAD PLAN:

- **Bewitching Gorp**—Make up to 7 days ahead; store at room temperature in a container with a tight-fitting lid.
- **Peanut-Butter & Jam Jack-O'-Lanterns**—Make dough up to 2 weeks ahead; refrigerate or freeze. Thaw frozen dough in refrigerator. Bake cookies up to 3 days ahead. Refrigerate in an airtight container.
- **Banana-Orange-Yogurt Cups**—Make up to 24 hours ahead.
- **Goblin's Drumsticks**—Bake up to 24 hours ahead.
- **Individual Cartons of Orange Juice or Orange Drink**—Refrigerate until just before guests arrive.

Short-Cuts:

- Purchase ready-cooked drumsticks.
- Serve commercial granola or trail mix instead of Bewitching Gorp.
- Limit refreshments to Peanut-Butter & Jam Jack-O'-Lanterns and orange juice or orange drink.

Goblin's Drumsticks
Photo on page 40.

Easy to make ahead with a coating that children love.

**1-1/2 cups finely crushed nacho-cheese-
  flavored corn chips (about 6 oz.)**
1 egg, lightly beaten

1/2 cup milk
12 chicken legs without thighs

Grease a 13″ x 9″ baking pan. Preheat oven to 350F (175C). Pour chips into a pie pan. In a shallow bowl, combine egg and milk. Dip chicken in egg mixture; then in chips. Place in a single layer in greased pan. Bake in preheated oven 45 minutes. Cool in pan 5 minutes. Place cooked chicken on a platter. Refrigerate 30 minutes or until cold. *Complete now or make ahead.*

To complete now, wrap individually in plastic wrap. Place 1 wrapped drumstick in each treat box. Refrigerate until guests arrive.

To make ahead, place baked chicken on a platter. Cover with foil or plastic wrap; refrigerate up to 24 hours. Wrap and serve as directed above. Makes 12 drumsticks.

Banana-Orange-Yogurt Cups
Photo on page 40.

No trick to make, but a real treat to eat.

1 (6-oz.) pkg. orange-flavored gelatin
2 cups boiling water

2 bananas
8 oz. plain yogurt (1 cup)

In a small bowl, dissolve gelatin in boiling water. In a medium bowl, mash 1 banana; stir in yogurt. Gradually stir dissolved gelatin into yogurt mixture. Pour into 10 to 12 (5- or 6-ounce) individual paper cups. Cover cups with lids or foil. *Complete now or make ahead.*

To complete now, refrigerate until firm. Slice remaining banana; use to garnish gelatin. Place 1 cup in each treat box. Refrigerate until guests arrive.

To make ahead, refrigerate up to 24 hours. Garnish and serve as directed above. Makes 10 to 12 servings.

Bewitching Gorp
Photo on pages 40 and 151.

Healthful combination of cereal and dried fruits.

1/2 cup shelled sunflower seeds
2 cups crispy rice cereal
1/4 cup shaved coconut
1/4 cup honey

2 tablespoons vegetable oil
1/2 teaspoon vanilla extract
1/2 cup golden raisins
1-1/2 cups chopped mixed dried fruit

Preheat oven to 325F (165C). In a 13″ x 9″ baking pan, combine seeds, cereal and coconut. In a small bowl, combine honey, oil and vanilla. Stir into cereal mixture. Bake in preheated oven 15 minutes, stirring occasionally. Stir in dried fruit. Cool to room temperature. *Complete now or make ahead.*

To complete now, spoon into 10 to 12 small plastic bags. Tie each with orange yarn or string. Place 1 bag in each treat box as guests arrive.

To make ahead, place in a container with a tight-fitting lid. Store at room temperature up to 7 days. Serve as directed above. Makes about 5 cups.

How to Make Peanut-Butter & Jam Jack-O'-Lanterns

1/Spread peanut butter over plain circles. Top each with 1 teaspoon jam.

2/In each Treat Box, place a Goblin's Drumstick, Banana-Orange-Yogurt Cup and Bewitching Gorp, all recipes on page 39. Add a drink to each box.

Peanut-Butter & Jam Jack-O'-Lanterns

Children's favorite flavors combined in an oatmeal cookie.

1/2 cup vegetable shortening
2/3 cup lightly packed brown sugar
1 egg
1 teaspoon vanilla extract
1/2 teaspoon baking soda

3/4 cup quick-cooking rolled oats
2 cups all-purpose flour
About 1/3 cup smooth or chunk-style
  peanut butter
About 1/3 cup strawberry jam

In a large bowl, beat shortening and brown sugar until fluffy. Beat in egg, vanilla and baking soda. Stir in oats and flour; shape into 2 balls. Wrap each in plastic wrap or foil. *Complete now or make ahead.*

To complete now, refrigerate 1 hour. Preheat oven to 375F (190C). Roll out 1/2 of dough until 1/8 inch thick. Cut into 16 (3-inch) circles, or cut with a jack-o'-lantern cutter. Spread each circle with 1 teaspoon peanut butter to within 1/2 inch of edge. Spread each with about 1 teaspoon jam. Roll out remaining dough 1/8 inch thick. Cut into 16 (3-inch) circles, or cut with a jack-o'-lantern cutter. Cut a jack-o'-lantern face in each circle. Place cut-out circles on top of jam-covered circles. Press edges to seal. Place sandwiched cookies on an ungreased baking sheet. Bake in preheated oven 10 minutes or until lightly browned. Remove from baking sheet; cool on a wire rack. Place 1 cookie in each treat box. Refrigerate until guests arrive. Serve cold.

To make ahead, refrigerate dough up to 2 days; freeze up to 2 weeks. Thaw frozen dough in re-frigerator overnight. To shape cookies, let dough stand at room temperature 15 minutes. Roll out, cut and bake cookies as directed above. Place cookies in a single layer in a container with a tight-fitting lid. Refrigerate up to 3 days. Makes 16 cookies.

New Twist to Thanksgiving

Thanksgiving Roll-Ups with Pistachio Stuffing
Stuffed Sweet Potatoes
Baked Sweet & Sour Onions
Golden-Grove Salad
Persimmon-Nut Bread
Pumpkin-Pecan Cheesecake

Are you tired of preparing the same foods in the same way every Thanksgiving? We love all the traditional flavors of Thanksgiving, but decided to vary a few of the dishes to make it easier on the host and hostess. Instead of the usual candied or mashed sweet potatoes, we like to bake them. Then we scoop the potatoes out of the shells, mash them with apples, spices and pork sausage and spoon them back into the shells. For a dramatic dash of brilliant color and wonderful flavor, include refreshing Golden-Grove Salad.

If you're thinking of a poultry dish on a smaller scale than traditional turkey, make Thanksgiving Roll-Ups with Pistachio Stuffing. If you want to serve two roll-ups per person, double the recipe. For dessert, try pumpkin in a spicy cheesecake that's loaded with pecans.

Best of all, these make-ahead recipes were designed to give you time to enjoy Thanksgiving. Although you may not be ready to break completely with tradition, we hope you will include several of these recipes at your next Thanksgiving dinner. Serves 8 people.

MAKE-AHEAD PLAN:

- **Thanksgiving Roll-Ups with Pistachio Stuffing**—Roll and freeze chicken breasts with dressing up to 1 month ahead. Thaw overnight in refrigerator. Or, make roll-ups and sauce up to 24 hours ahead; refrigerate. Bake during final 30 to 40 minutes onions bake.
- **Persimmon-Nut Bread**—Make up to 7 days ahead; wrap airtight and store in refrigerator. Bring to room temperature before cutting. Flavor improves if let stand at least 24 hours.
- **Pumpkin-Pecan Cheesecake**—Make up to 24 hours ahead. Let cool before refrigerating.
- **Baked Sweet & Sour Onions**—Stuff up to 24 hours ahead. Bake just before serving.
- **Stuffed Sweet Potatoes**—Bake and stuff potatoes up to 24 hours ahead. Heat during final 30 minutes onions bake.
- **Golden-Grove Salad**—Section grapefruit and orange up to 24 hours ahead. Make dressing up to 24 hours ahead, but do not combine with fruit. Finish salad about 1 hour before serving.

Short-Cuts:
- Serve plain baked or mashed sweet potatoes.
- Use a sweet-sour commercial French-style salad dressing with Golden-Grove Salad.

Thanksgiving Roll-Ups with Pistachio Stuffing

A regal way to turn chicken breasts into a memorable dish.

8 chicken-breast halves, boned, skinned
2 tablespoons butter or margarine
6 medium mushrooms, chopped
1/4 cup chopped pistachios
1/2 cup chopped cooked ham
1/2 cup soft bread crumbs

1/2 teaspoon salt
1/8 teaspoon pepper
3 or 4 thin orange slices
Parsley sprig
Whole shelled pistachios, if desired

White-Wine Sauce:
2 teaspoons cornstarch
1/2 cup dry white wine
1/4 cup butter or margarine, melted

1/4 cup apricot preserves
1/4 cup fruit chutney, chopped

Place chicken-breast halves, 1 at a time, between 2 pieces of waxed paper or plastic wrap. Using side of a meat mallet, lightly pound chicken breasts to an even thickness; set aside. In a small skillet, melt 2 tablespoons butter or margarine. Add mushrooms, chopped pistachios and ham. Sauté until mushrooms are tender. Stir in bread crumbs. Sprinkle pounded chicken breasts with salt and pepper. Spoon equal amounts of bread-crumb mixture across center of each breast; roll up, jelly-roll style. Secure with wooden picks, if desired. *Complete now or make ahead.*

To complete now, preheat oven to 350F (175C). Make White-Wine Sauce; spoon over roll-ups. Bake 30 to 40 minutes in preheated oven until chicken is tender. Spoon sauce over chicken rolls at least once during baking. Roll-ups may be baked during final 30 to 40 minutes onions bake. To serve, arrange baked roll-ups on a platter or serving plate. Spoon any remaining sauce over rolls. Garnish with orange slices, parsley sprig and whole pistachios, if desired. Serve hot.

To make White-Wine Sauce, in a small saucepan, combine cornstarch and wine, stirring until smooth. Stir in butter or margarine, apricot preserves and chutney. Stirring constantly, cook over medium-low heat until translucent.

To make ahead, place stuffed rolls, seam-side down, in a 13″ x 9″ baking pan. Cover with foil or plastic wrap; refrigerate up to 24 hours. Or, place stuffed roll-ups, seam-side down, on a baking sheet. Freeze until firm. Wrap frozen roll-ups airtight in freezer wrap. Store in freezer up to 1 month. Thaw overnight in refrigerator. Make sauce up to 24 hours ahead; store in a container with a tight-fitting lid. Bake 40 to 50 minutes; garnish and serve as directed above. Makes 4 to 8 servings.

How to Make Thanksgiving Roll-Ups

1/Spoon filling onto chicken breasts. Roll up; place seam-side down in baking pan.

2/Garnish with whole pistachios and orange slices, if desired. Serve hot.

Baked Sweet & Sour Onions

A change-of-pace vegetable dish that complements poultry or pork.

2 bacon slices, diced
4 large onions, peeled, halved crosswise
2 tablespoons red-wine vinegar
2 tablespoons brown sugar

1/2 teaspoon Dijon-style mustard
1/2 teaspoon salt
1/8 teaspoon pepper

In a large skillet, cook bacon until crisp. Use a slotted spoon to remove cooked bacon from skillet; set aside. Place onions, cut-side down, in skillet with bacon drippings. Brown over medium heat; turn cut-side up. Brown other side. Place onions, cut-side up, in an ungreased, shallow 11" x 7" baking dish. Spoon pan drippings over onions. In a small bowl, combine vinegar, brown sugar, mustard, salt and pepper; spoon over onions. Sprinkle tops of onions with reserved cooked bacon. *Complete now or make ahead.*

To complete now, preheat oven to 350F (175C). Bake 35 to 40 minutes or until onions are tender. Use slotted spoon to place baked onions in a serving dish; pour pan drippings over tops of onions. Serve hot.

To make ahead, cover with foil or plastic wrap; refrigerate up to 24 hours. About 1 hour before serving, remove cover; place pan in cold oven. Turn oven to 350F (175C). Bake 45 to 50 minutes or until onions are tender. Serve as directed above. Makes 8 servings.

Golden-Grove Salad

It's impressive looking, wonderful tasting and one of our favorite recipes.

2 tablespoons white-wine vinegar
1 teaspoon lemon juice
3 tablespoons sugar
1/2 teaspoon grated onion
1/4 teaspoon salt
1/4 teaspoon dry mustard
1/8 teaspoon paprika

1/3 cup vegetable oil
1 teaspoon celery seeds
2 large oranges
2 medium grapefruit
Lettuce leaves
1 ripe avocado
2 to 3 tablespoons pomegranate seeds

In a blender or food processor fitted with a metal blade, combine vinegar, lemon juice, sugar, onion, salt, dry mustard and paprika. Process until blended. With machine running, gradually pour in vegetable oil until well blended. Add celery seeds; set aside. Peel oranges and grapefruit, removing colored peel and white pith. Cut on each side of membrane dividing sections; carefully lift out sections of fruit. *Complete now or make ahead.*

To complete now, arrange lettuce leaves in a deep platter. Peel and slice avocado. On lettuce-lined platter, arrange avocado slices alternately with orange sections and grapefruit sections. Sprinkle pomegranate seeds over fruit slices. Spoon dressing over fruit, or serve dressing separately.

To make ahead, place orange and grapefruit sections in a shallow dish. Cover with foil or plastic wrap. Pour dressing into a container with a tight-fitting lid. Refrigerate fruit and dressing separately up to 24 hours. Serve as directed above. Makes about 8 servings.

Stuffed Sweet Potatoes

The flavor is superb!

4 large sweet potatoes or yams
1/2 lb. bulk pork sausage
1 cooking apple, peeled, cored, chopped
1/4 teaspoon ground cinnamon

1/2 teaspoon grated orange peel
2 tablespoons maple syrup
2 tablespoons butter, melted
1/4 cup chopped walnuts

Preheat oven to 400F (205C). Place potatoes in a 9-inch-square baking pan. Bake in preheated oven 50 to 60 minutes or until tender when pricked with a fork. Cut each in half lengthwise. Scoop out pulp into a medium bowl, leaving a 1/4-inch layer of pulp inside each shell. Mash scooped-out pulp; set aside. In a medium saucepan or skillet, sauté sausage until some of fat is rendered out. Remove rendered fat from pan. Add apple to partially cooked sausage; sauté over medium heat until apple is tender and sausage is no longer pink. Pour into a sieve to drain. Add drained sausage mixture to mashed sweet-potato pulp. Stir in cinnamon, orange peel and maple syrup. Spoon into sweet-potato shells. Grease a 13'' x 9'' baking pan; arrange stuffed shells in pan. *Complete now or make ahead.*

To complete now, reduce oven temperature to 350F (175C). Brush tops of stuffed potatoes with melted butter. Sprinkle walnuts on top. Bake in preheated oven 30 minutes. Place on a platter or serving plate; serve hot.

To make ahead, cover with foil or plastic wrap; refrigerate up to 24 hours. Top with melted butter and walnuts. Bake and serve as directed above. Makes 8 servings.

Pumpkin-Pecan Cheesecake

If you want to enhance your reputation as a cook, here's your chance!

1-1/2 cups graham-cracker crumbs
1 tablespoon sugar
1/4 cup butter, melted
1/3 cup finely chopped pecans
2 (8-oz.) pkgs. cream cheese,
  room temperature
3/4 cup sugar
3 eggs
1/2 cup whipping cream

1 cup canned pumpkin
2 tablespoons maple syrup
1/2 teaspoon ground ginger
1/2 teaspoon ground cinnamon
1/4 teaspoon ground nutmeg
1/2 pint dairy sour cream (1 cup)
3 tablespoons sugar
1/4 teaspoon vanilla extract
1/3 cup pecan halves

In a medium bowl, combine graham-cracker crumbs, 1 tablespoon sugar, butter and chopped pecans. Press over bottom and about 1-1/2 inches up side of an ungreased 9-inch springform pan; refrigerate. Preheat oven to 325F (165C). In a large bowl, beat cream cheese and 3/4 cup sugar until light and fluffy. Beat in eggs and whipping cream. Stir in pumpkin, maple syrup and spices. Pour into chilled crust. Bake in preheated oven 55 to 60 minutes. In a small bowl, combine sour cream, 3 tablespoons sugar and vanilla. Stir until blended. Spread over hot cheesecake. Arrange pecan halves over top. Bake 10 minutes. Let stand until cool. *Complete now or make ahead.*

To complete now, refrigerate at least 4 hours. To serve, remove side of pan. Cut cheesecake into wedges; serve on indiviudal plates.

To make ahead, cover cooled cheesecake with foil or plastic wrap. Refrigerate up to 4 days. Serve as directed above. Makes 8 to 10 servings.

●●●

Persimmon-Nut Bread

It's even better the second day.

2 ripe persimmons
1 tablespoon lemon juice
3/4 cup sugar
1/3 cup vegetable oil
2 eggs, lightly beaten
1/3 cup milk
1-3/4 cups all-purpose flour

1 teaspoon baking soda
1/2 teaspoon baking powder
1/2 teaspoon salt
1/2 teaspoon ground cinnamon
1/4 teaspoon ground cloves
1/2 cup chopped walnuts

Grease a 9" x 5" loaf pan. Preheat oven to 350F (175C). Cut persimmons crosswise; remove and discard seeds. Scoop out pulp. In a blender or food processor fitted with a metal blade, process pulp and lemon juice until pureed; set aside. In a large bowl, beat sugar, oil, eggs, milk and persimmon puree until combined. In a medium bowl, blend flour, baking soda, baking powder, salt, cinnamon, cloves and walnuts. Stir flour mixture into persimmon mixture. Spoon into greased pan. Bake in preheated oven 50 to 60 minutes or until a wooden pick inserted in center comes out clean. Turn out onto a wire rack to cool. *Complete now or make ahead.*

To complete now, cool completely before slicing. Arrange slices on a platter or serving plate. To serve warm, reheat 15 minutes in a 350F (175C) oven.

To make ahead, bake up to 7 days ahead. Cool and wrap airtight in foil or plastic wrap; refrigerate or freeze up to 7 days. Serve as directed above. Makes 1 loaf.

Greet the Festive Season

Holiday Vegetable Tidbits
Star-of-Endive Salad
Regal-Crown Pork Roast
Orange-Spiced Figs
Mushrooms au Gratin
Green Beans Primo
Dinner Rolls
Frozen Lemon-Macaroon Cream

'Tis the season to be jolly—and the season when you feast on an array of traditional holiday fare. Everyone looks forward to lavish holiday menus, the glow of candlelight and the sparkle of Christmas decorations.

As guests arrive, serve a tray of colorful Holiday Vegetable Tidbits to go with your favorite aperitif. Then, for a dramatic effect, serve Star-of-Endive Salad on individual plates before serving the main course.

At this elegant dinner party, even the dessert is luxurious. The tangy freshness of Frozen Lemon-Macaroon Cream gives the right finishing touch. Serves 6 or 7 people.

MAKE-AHEAD PLAN:

- **Holiday Vegetable Tidbits**—Make cheese mixture 2 to 3 days ahead.
- **Frozen Lemon-Macaroon Cream**—Make and freeze 2 to 3 days ahead.
- **Orange-Spiced Figs**—Make up to 24 hours ahead.
- **Green Beans Primo**—Make up to 24 hours ahead. Heat at serving time.
- **Regal-Crown Pork Roast**—Make stuffing up to 24 hours ahead. About 4 hours before serving, stuff and bake pork. See Mushrooms au Gratin, below.
- **Mushrooms au Gratin**—Make up to 24 hours ahead. If you have only 1 oven, roast pork 1/2 hour ahead of schedule. Remove from oven; cover with foil while mushrooms heat.
- **Star-of-Endive Salad**—Mix dressing and sliced leaves up to 12 hours ahead.

Short-Cuts:

- This is a very elegant dinner and will not have the same effect if short-cuts are taken.

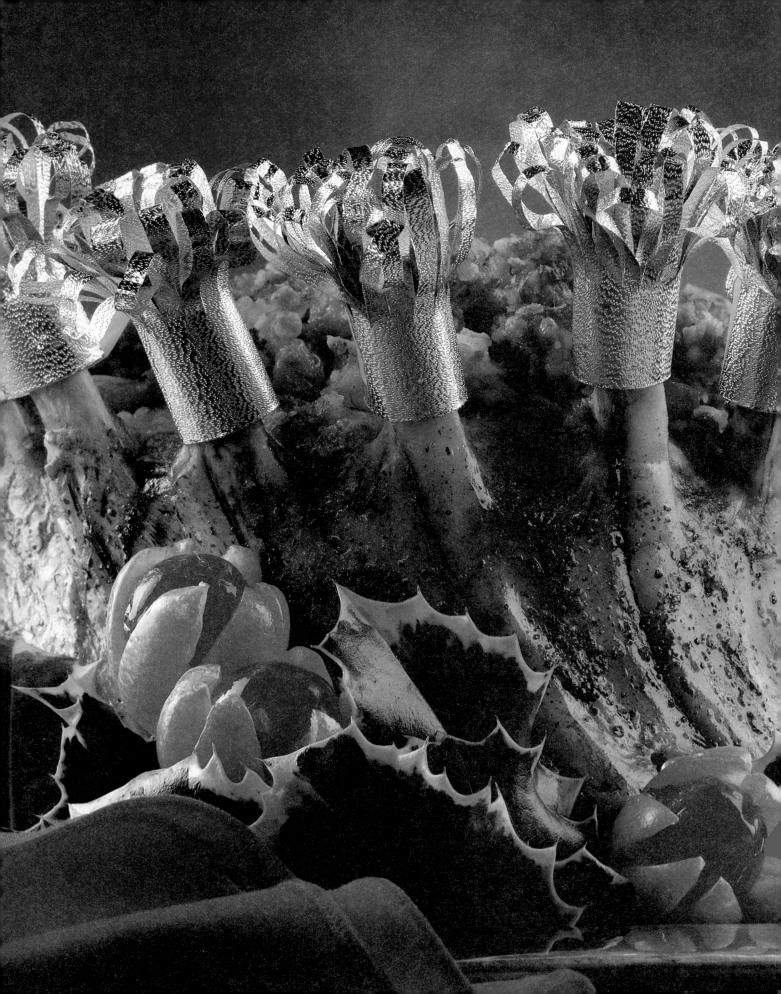

Greet the Festive Season

The perfect feature for holiday fare is Regal-Crown Pork Roast, filled with a savory sausage mixture studded with morsels of spicy fruits and nuts. Serve it on your most handsome tray, garnished with cherry-stuffed kumquats and artificial holly.

Regal-Crown Pork Roast, page 50

Regal-Crown Pork Roast

Photo on pages 48-49.

This special cut of meat is designed for very special events in your life.

1/2 cup golden raisins	1/2 cup soft bread crumbs
1/4 cup orange-flavored liqueur	1 egg, lightly beaten
3/4 lb. bulk pork sausage	Salt
1 small onion, chopped	Pepper
1 medium apple, peeled, cored, diced	1 (7- to 8-lb.) crown-rib pork roast
1/2 cup chopped walnuts	Kumquats
1/4 teaspoon ground cinnamon	Maraschino cherries
1/2 teaspoon grated orange peel	

In a small bowl, combine raisins and liqueur; set aside. Crumble sausage into a large skillet. Add onion; sauté until onion is soft and sausage is no longer pink. Drain, discarding excess fat. Stir in apple, walnuts, cinnamon, orange peel, bread crumbs and reserved raisin mixture. Stir in egg. *Complete now or make ahead.*

To complete now, preheat oven to 325F (165C). Salt and pepper roast inside and outside; place on a broiler pan. Lightly spoon stuffing into cavity of roast. Loosely cover stuffing and tips of bones with foil. Bake in preheated oven 3-1/2 to 4 hours or until a meat thermometer inserted in thickest part of meat reaches 170F (75C). Place roast on a platter or serving plate. Place gold or silver paper frills on ends of bones. Cut kumquats as shown; stuff with maraschino cherries. Use to garnish roast. To serve, spoon stuffing out of center; carve between ribs.

To make ahead, cover and refrigerate stuffing up to 24 hours. Stuff roast; bake, garnish and serve as directed above. Makes 6 or 7 servings of 2 ribs each.

●●●

Mushrooms au Gratin

Teams up well with any kind of meat.

1/4 cup butter or margarine	1/4 teaspoon salt
2 green onions, chopped	1/8 teaspoon pepper
1/4 cup all-purpose flour	1/2 cup dairy sour cream
1 lb. medium mushrooms, quartered	1/2 cup soft bread crumbs
1 cup chicken broth or bouillon	1/4 cup grated Parmesan cheese
1 teaspoon Worcestershire sauce	

In a large skillet, melt butter or margarine. Add green onions; sauté until soft. Sprinkle flour over onions. Stirring constantly, cook 2 minutes. Stir in mushrooms, broth or bouillon, Worcestershire sauce, salt and pepper. Simmer, stirring constantly, 4 to 5 minutes or until thickened. Remove from heat; stir in sour cream. Pour into a shallow baking dish. In a small bowl, combine bread crumbs and cheese; sprinkle over mushroom mixture. *Complete now or make ahead.*

To complete now, preheat oven to 350F (175C). Bake 20 to 25 minutes or until bubbly; serve in baking dish. Serve hot.

To make ahead, cover with foil or plastic wrap; refrigerate up to 24 hours. About 30 minutes before serving, remove cover. Place dish in cold oven. Turn oven to 350F (175C). Bake 30 minutes or until bubbly. Serve hot. Makes 6 to 8 servings.

How to Make Holiday Vegetable Tidbits

1/Cut cherry tomatoes in half; scoop out centers. Slice zucchini.

2/Spoon cheese mixture into tomato halves and onto zucchini slices. Garnish as shown.

Holiday Vegetable Tidbits

Colorful red and green appetizers that are as nutritious as they are delicious.

1 (4-oz.) pkg. blue cheese or
  Roquefort cheese
1 (3-oz.) pkg. cream cheese,
  room temperature
1/2 teaspoon Worcestershire sauce
2 teaspoons minced fresh chives or
  green onion
1/8 teaspoon salt

1/8 teaspoon pepper
3 tablespoons dairy sour cream
1/2 teaspoon Dijon-style mustard
16 cherry tomatoes
1 large zucchini
Chopped green onion or chopped parsley
Pimento strips

In a small bowl or in a food processor fitted with a metal blade, beat or process blue cheese or Roquefort cheese, cream cheese, Worcestershire sauce, minced chives or green onions, salt, pepper, sour cream and mustard until blended. *Complete now or make ahead.*

To complete now, cut off tops of cherry tomatoes. Scoop out centers; use for another purpose. Invert tomato shells on paper towels to drain 15 to 20 minutes. Spoon about 1-1/2 teaspoons cheese mixture into each drained tomato. Garnish tops with chopped green onions or chopped parsley. Cut zucchini into 16 crosswise slices; mound 1 level teaspoon cheese mixture on each zucchini slice. Garnish zucchini slices with a pimento strip. Serve on a platter or serving plate.

To make ahead, prepare cheese mixture 2 to 3 days ahead. Spoon into a container with a tight-fitting lid; refrigerate. About 3-1/2 hours before serving, prepare vegetables. Fill or top vegetables with cheese mixture; refrigerate up to 3 hours. Garnish and serve as directed above. Makes 32 appetizer tidbits.

Star-of-Endive Salad

A dramatic presentation to impress your guests.

5 Belgian-endive heads
1/4 lb. medium mushrooms, sliced
1 tablespoon chopped pimento
1/3 cup mayonnaise
1 teaspoon Dijon-style mustard
1 tablespoon minced chives
2 tablespoons minced watercress leaves

1/4 teaspoon salt
1/8 teaspoon pepper
1/4 teaspoon dried leaf chervil, crushed
2 tablespoons olive oil or vegetable oil
2 tablespoons tarragon vinegar
1 tablespoon lemon juice

Remove 30 to 35 of largest outside endive leaves. Place large leaves in a plastic bag; refrigerate. Cut remaining endive into 1/4-inch crosswise slices. In a large bowl, combine sliced endive, mushrooms and pimento. In a small bowl, combine mayonnaise, mustard, chives, watercress, salt, pepper, chervil, oil, vinegar and lemon juice. Pour over mushroom mixture; toss to coat. Cover with foil or plastic wrap. *Complete now or make ahead.*

To complete now, refrigerate mushroom mixture 2 hours to let flavors blend. To serve, arrange 5 reserved leaves on each luncheon plate. Spoon salad mixture onto lined plates.

To make ahead, refrigerate up to 12 hours. Serve as directed above. Makes 6 or 7 servings.

Orange-Spiced Figs

Serve as an accompaniment to roast pork or chicken.

1/2 cup sugar
1/2 cup red-wine vinegar
3/4 cup water
1 (3-inch) cinnamon stick

6 whole cloves
1 small orange, unpeeled
1 lb. fresh figs (12 to 15)

In a medium saucepan, combine sugar, vinegar, water, cinnamon stick and cloves. Cut orange into 6 or 7 crosswise slices; cut each slice in half. Add to vinegar mixture. Bring to a boil; simmer 5 minutes. Remove fig stems; place figs in a 1-1/2-quart heatproof bowl. Pour boiling syrup over figs. Cover with foil or plastic wrap. Let stand at room temperature about 30 minutes. *Complete now or make ahead.*

To complete now, drain; place figs around meat or in a serving bowl.

To make ahead, refrigerate figs in marinade up to 24 hours. Serve as directed above. Makes 12 to 15 spiced figs.

Green Beans Primo

An easy make-ahead dish that heats in minutes on the stovetop.

1 (20-oz.) pkg. frozen French-style green
   beans or 1-1/2 lbs. fresh green beans,
   cut in julienne strips
2 tablespoons soy sauce
1 tablespoon vegetable oil
1 teaspoon sesame oil

1/4 cup sherry
1 garlic clove, crushed
1 teaspoon cornstarch
1 (8-oz.) can whole water chestnuts,
   drained, sliced

Cook beans in lightly salted water 6 to 8 minutes or until crisp-tender; drain. In a large skillet, combine soy sauce, vegetable oil, sesame oil, sherry and garlic. Stir in cornstarch; stirring constantly, cook until thickened. Gently stir in water chestnuts and cooked beans until hot and coated with sauce. *Complete now or make ahead.*

To complete now, spoon into a serving bowl; serve hot.

To make ahead, spoon into a medium bowl. Cover with foil or plastic wrap; refrigerate up to 24 hours. Reheat before serving. Serve as directed above. Makes 6 to 8 servings.

Frozen Lemon-Macaroon Cream

A refreshingly tart, yet slightly chewy, grand finale to your special dinner.

4 eggs, separated
1 cup sugar
1/2 cup lemon juice
1/2 teaspoon grated lemon peel
3/4 lb. soft, chewy coconut macaroons

1/4 teaspoon cream of tartar
1/2 pint whipping cream (1 cup)
Whipped cream, if desired
Candied cherries, if desired

In a small bowl, beat egg yolks and 1/2 cup sugar until thickened, about 5 minutes. Pour into a 1-1/2-quart saucepan. Stir in lemon juice and lemon peel. Stirring constantly, cook over very low heat until mixture thickens. Set aside to cool. Break macaroons into 1/2-inch pieces. Reserve 1 cup macaroon pieces. Line bottom and about 1 inch up side of an 8-inch springform pan with remaining macaroon pieces. In a medium bowl, beat egg whites and cream of tartar until foamy. Gradually add remaining 1/2 cup sugar, beating until thick and glossy. Fold beaten egg whites and reserved macaroon pieces into cooled lemon mixture. Beat 1 cup whipping cream until soft peaks form; fold into lemon mixture. Carefully spoon into macaroon-lined pan. *Complete now or make ahead.*

To complete now, freeze at least 4 hours or until firm. To serve, remove foil and side of pan. Cut frozen mixture into wedges; place wedges on individual plates. Garnish each serving with a dollop of whipped cream and a candied cherry, if desired.

To make ahead, cover with foil; freeze 2 to 3 days. Garnish and serve as directed above. Makes 6 to 8 servings.

Shower Her With Best Wishes

Champagne
Honey-Roasted Nuts
Tarragon Eggs
Golden-State Chicken Loaf
International Appetizer Cutouts
Cinnamon-Apple Salad
Strawberry Ice-Cream Heart Cake

Your best friend is engaged and you're planning a bridal shower for her. With your busy schedule, you must plan the make-ahead food carefully so everything will be ready on time. Limit the guests to 12 people or double the recipes. If it is important to increase the guest list, enlist the aid of friends or neighbors to help with storage of perishables.

Set the mood to celebrate with a champagne toast to the guest of honor. Serve the foods cold except International Appetizer Cutouts. Heat the appetizers and serve on a hot tray at the end of the table where they will be the last food taken. This will help to keep them hot.

Strawberry Ice-Cream Heart Cake is the most glamorous part of the menu. If necessary, make two identical heart cakes. Arrange them side by side on a large tray for a dramatic presentation. Because the cake is filled with ice cream, bring it to the table when you're ready to serve dessert. Serves 10 to 12 people.

MAKE-AHEAD PLAN:

- **International Appetizer Cutouts**—Prepare and freeze up to 6 weeks ahead.
- **Honey-Roasted Nuts**—Make up to 7 days ahead. Store at room temperature.
- **Strawberry Ice-Cream Heart Cake**—Bake cake up to 7 days ahead; freeze. Make ice-cream layer in same pan cake is baked in. Freeze up to 24 hours or until firm. Assemble cake and ice-cream layers 2 hours before frosting with whipped cream. Freeze frosted cake 2 to 3 hours or until firm. Rinse and dry strawberries 2 to 3 hours before serving. Place cake in refrigerator 15 minutes before serving to soften slightly; add strawberries seconds before serving.
- **Golden-State Chicken Loaf**—Bake up to 24 hours before party; serve warm or cold.
- **Cinnamon-Apple Salad**—Make and refrigerate up to 24 hours ahead.
- **Tarragon Eggs**—Cook eggs up to 24 hours before party. Fill eggs 2 to 3 hours before serving.
- **Champagne**—Refrigerate 3 to 4 hours. Serve at 40F to 45F (5C).

Short-Cuts:

- Serve champagne, Strawberry-Ice-Cream Heart Cake and Honey-Roasted Nuts. Or, serve Tarragon Eggs and International Appetizer Cutouts before the cake is cut.

Honey-Roasted Nuts

Mixed nuts are enhanced by a spicy honey glaze.

2 tablespoons honey
1/4 teaspoon ground cinnamon
1/4 teaspoon ground mace

1 tablespoon butter or margarine, melted
1 (12-oz.) can mixed salted nuts

Preheat oven to 325F (165C). In a medium bowl, combine honey, cinnamon, mace and butter or margarine. Add mixed nuts; toss to coat. Spread in a 15″ x 10″ jelly-roll pan. Bake in preheated oven 10 minutes, stirring at least once. Cool to room temperature. *Complete now or make ahead.*

To complete now, serve in a decorative serving bowl.

To make ahead, spoon cooled nuts into a container with a tight-fitting lid. Store at room temperature up to 7 days. Serve as directed above. Makes about 2-1/2 cups.

Tarragon Eggs

These have a bit more flair and flavor than traditional deviled eggs.

12 hard-cooked eggs
1/2 cup butter or margarine, melted
1 cup diced cooked chicken or turkey
2 tablespoons half and half
4 teaspoons chopped fresh tarragon leaves

2 teaspoons wine vinegar
1/2 teaspoon salt
1/4 teaspoon pepper
Tarragon leaves

Peel eggs; cut in half lengthwise. Remove hard-cooked egg yolks from whites; set egg whites aside. In a blender or food processor fitted with a metal blade, combine hard-cooked egg yolks, butter or margarine, chicken or turkey, half and half, chopped tarragon, vinegar, salt and pepper. Process until mixture is smooth. *Complete now or make ahead.*

To complete now, mound egg-yolk mixture into egg-white halves. Or, spoon egg-yolk mixture into a pastry bag; pipe into egg-white halves. Garnish with tarragon leaves; arrange on a small platter or serving plate. Serve cold.

To make ahead, place cooked egg whites and egg-yolk mixture in separate containers with tight-fitting lids. Refrigerate up to 24 hours. Assemble and serve as directed above. Makes 24 appetizers.

Fresh Vegetable Nosegay

For a lovely centerpiece, make a Vegetable Nosegay. Purchase the base of nosegay from a party shop or floral-supply store. Insert small wooden picks into each vegetable piece. Arrange the following vegetables in concentric circles from outside to center by inserting wooden picks into foam in nosegay base: diagonally sliced peeled carrots; peeled turnip slices, halved; radish roses; broccoli flowerets in center.

Add other vegetables as desired. Tuck pieces of leaf lettuce around outside edge, letting some of lace show.

Golden-State Chicken Loaf

It's equally good served hot or cold.

2 cups cubed, smoked, boneless chicken or
    turkey
1/3 cup toasted almonds
2 tablespoons chopped green onions
1/4 cup butter
1/4 cup all-purpose flour
1/2 pint half and half (1 cup)
3 eggs, separated
1/2 cup chicken broth or bouillon

1/2 teaspoon dried leaf tarragon, crushed
1/2 teaspoon salt
1/8 teaspoon pepper
1/2 teaspoon Dijon-style mustard
2 tablespoons white wine
About 36 asparagus spears, cooked
5 thin carrot slices
Fresh tarragon sprigs, if desired

Grease a 9" x 5" loaf pan; set aside. In a food processor fitted with a metal blade, combine chicken or turkey, almonds and green onions. Process until finely chopped but not pureed; set aside. In a small saucepan, melt butter; stir in flour. Stirring constantly, cook about 2 minutes. Stir in half and half; continue stirring until smooth and thick. Remove sauce from heat; set aside. In a medium bowl, beat egg yolks until blended; stir in broth or bouillon. In a large bowl, combine chicken or turkey mixture, egg-yolk mixture and sauce. Stir in dried tarragon, salt, pepper, mustard and wine. Beat egg whites until stiff but not dry; fold into combined mixture. Arrange 1/2 of asparagus spears crosswise in greased loaf pan, cutting stems to fit. Spoon 1/2 of chicken mixture over asparagus spears. Arrange remaining asparagus spears crosswise over top, again cutting to fit; then spoon in remaining chicken mixture. *Complete now or make ahead.*

To complete now, preheat oven to 350F (175C). Place loaf pan in a 13" x 9" baking pan; place both pans in preheated oven. Pour boiling water about 1 inch deep in outer pan. Bake 55 to 65 minutes or until a knife inserted in center comes out clean. Remove from hot water; let stand at least 5 minutes on a rack. Loosen from sides of pan with a small spatula; invert onto a platter or serving plate. Remove pan. Using an hors d'oeuvre cutter, cut carrot slices into flower shapes. Use to garnish top of loaf. Garnish platter or serving plate with fresh tarragon sprigs, if desired. Slice and serve warm. Or cool; refrigerate until chilled. Slice and serve cold.

To make ahead, cover unbaked mixture with foil or plastic wrap; refrigerate up to 24 hours. About 2 hours before serving, remove cover. Bake as directed above for 1 hour and 15 minutes or until a knife inserted in center comes out clean. Let cool; refrigerate until served. Or, immediately bake as directed above. Cool; leave in pan or remove from pan. Cover with foil or plastic wrap; refrigerate up to 24 hours. Reheat about 15 minutes in a 350F (175C) oven. Garnish and serve as directed above. Makes 15 to 18 servings.

How to Make Golden-State Chicken Loaf

1/Layer 1/2 of asparagus spears crosswise in pan. Top with 1/2 of chicken mixture. Repeat layers.

2/Bake; invert onto a platter. Garnish with carrot flowers and fresh tarragon, if desired.

Cinnamon-Apple Salad

Tastes as great as it looks!

2/3 cup cold water
3 (1/4-oz.) envelopes unflavored gelatin
   (3 tablespoons)
1-1/2 cups apple juice
1 cup red cinnamon candies

3 cups applesauce
3/4 cup dairy sour cream
Lettuce leaves
1 (14-oz.) jar spiced crab apples, drained

Pour water into a 1-cup measuring cup. Sprinkle gelatin over water; set aside to soften, 3 minutes. Pour apple juice into a medium saucepan; add candies. Stir over medium heat until candies dissolve. Add softened gelatin; stir until dissolved. Remove from heat; stir in applesauce. Pour 1/2 of applesauce mixture into a 6-cup gelatin mold. Reserve remaining applesauce mixture at room temperature. Refrigerate mixture in mold about 1-1/2 hours or until almost firm but still sticky on top. Stir sour cream into reserved applesauce mixture. Spoon over partially set gelatin. Cover with foil or plastic wrap. *Complete now or make ahead.*

To complete now, refrigerate 4 hours or until firm. Line a serving plate with lettuce leaves. Invert molded mixture onto lettuce-lined plate; remove mold. Garnish with spiced crab apples.

To make ahead, refrigerate up to 24 hours. Garnish and serve as directed above. Makes 10 to 12 servings.

How to Make Strawberry Ice-Cream Heart Cake

1/Invert ice-cream layer onto a cake layer; remove plastic.

2/Decorate cake with whipped cream mixture and fresh strawberries.

International Appetizer Cutouts

Choose a cutout design to match the theme of your party.

14 to 18 thin slices sandwich bread
1-1/2 to 2 tablespoons butter or margarine,
   room temperature
1 cup shredded Jarlsberg cheese (4 oz.)
2 bacon slices, cooked crisp, crumbled

1 green onion, chopped
1 fresh or canned green chili, chopped, or
   2 tablespoons canned diced green chilies
1/4 cup mayonnaise
5 or 6 cherry tomatoes, each cut into 3 slices

Cut bread into hearts, diamonds, triangles, circles or other shapes using 1-1/2- to 3-inch cookie cutters. Toast 1 side of each bread cutout. Thinly spread butter or margarine on untoasted sides. In a blender or food processor fitted with a metal blade, combine cheese, bacon, green onion, green chili and mayonnaise. Process until blended but not pureed. Spread 2 to 3 teaspoons of cheese mixture on buttered side of each cutout. *Complete now or make ahead.*

To complete now, place appetizer cutouts in a single layer on an ungreased baking sheet. Preheat broiler. Broil 5 to 6 inches from heat 2 to 4 minutes or until puffed and golden. Top each with a slice of cherry tomato. Arrange on a platter or serving plate; serve warm.

To make ahead, place appetizer cutouts in a single layer on an ungreased baking sheet; freeze. Place frozen appetizers in a plastic freezer bag or in a rigid container; seal. Freeze 1 to 6 weeks. Broil appetizers while frozen. Serve as directed above. Makes 14 to 18 appetizers.

Strawberry Ice-Cream Heart Cake

Guaranteed to be one of the most impressive cakes you'll ever serve.

2 cups all-purpose flour
1-1/2 cups sugar
1/2 cup vegetable shortening
1 cup milk
1 tablespoon baking powder
1/2 teaspoon salt
1 teaspoon vanilla extract
4 eggs

1 qt. strawberry ice cream, slightly
 softened
1/2 pint whipping cream (1 cup)
2 or 3 drops red food coloring, if desired
1 tablespoon black-raspberry liqueur,
 if desired
1 pint strawberries or raspberries (2 cups)

Grease and flour 2 (9-inch) heart-shaped cake pans. Preheat oven to 350F (175C). In a large bowl, combine flour, sugar, shortening, milk, baking powder, salt and vanilla. Beat on low speed with an electric mixer until blended. Increase to medium speed; beat about 30 seconds. Add eggs; beat 3 minutes. Spoon evenly into prepared pans. Bake in preheated oven 25 to 30 minutes or until a wooden pick inserted in center comes out clean. Cool in pan 5 minutes. Invert onto wire racks; remove pans. Let cool completely. *Complete now or make ahead.*

To complete now, wash and dry 1 heart-shaped cake pan. Line bottom and side of pan with plastic wrap. Press ice cream into lined pan; freeze 4 hours. Place 1 cake layer, bottom-side up, on a platter or serving plate. Invert ice cream onto bottom of cake layer; remove plastic wrap. Top with remaining cake layer, top-side up; freeze 2 hours. Whip cream; beat in food coloring and liqueur, if desired. Quickly spread a thin layer of whipped-cream mixture around side of cake. Spoon remaining whipped-cream mixture into a pastry bag fitted with a star tip. If ice cream or whipped-cream mixture becomes soft, place frosted cake in freezer until firm. Make a whipped-cream ruffle around base of cake. Make a lattice design across top; then a ruffle around top edge of cake. Freeze 2 to 3 hours or until firm. Cut large stawberries in half; use small strawberries whole. About 15 minutes before serving, place a strawberry or raspberry in center of each diamond in lattice design. Place several strawberries or raspberries in cream around base, if desired. Trim plate with small pink rosebuds and baby's breath, if desired. Refrigerate no longer than 10 minutes. Serve slices barely thawed.

To make ahead, wrap cake layers airtight with freezer wrap; freeze up to 7 days. About 3 days before party, line bottom and side of a 9-inch heart-shaped cake pan with plastic wrap. Press ice cream into pan; cover and freeze up to 24 hours. Invert ice cream onto bottom of 1 cake layer; remove plastic wrap. Top with remaining cake layer, top-side up. Decorate cake as directed above. Return frosted cake to freezer; freeze 2 to 3 hours or until firm. When firm, cover with plastic wrap or foil; store in freezer up to 24 hours. Serve as directed above. Makes about 12 servings.

Impressing the V.I.P.

Summer-Harvest Soup
Raspberry-Sauced Chicken Breasts
Golden-Glow Bake
Leeks Mimosa
Herbed Chèvre-Cheese Bread
Peachy Almond Pizza

News that a high-level executive from the home office is coming to town may create panic when it's first announced. After the first shock wave subsides, concentrate on ways to impress such an influential person. How about a beautifully orchestrated dinner party? It never fails to win admiration and appreciation.

Limit the number of guests so you can handle them and the dinner without hassle and overcrowding. If possible, make it a sit-down dinner for 6 to 8 people.

Obviously, all foods should be made ahead with a minimum of last-minute cooking and final touches. Plan to prepare most dishes the day or evening before.

Guests will be guessing the ingredients in rich smooth Summer-Harvest Soup. Then your reputation as a culinary authority will increase as everyone tastes Raspberry-Sauced Chicken Breasts and the other tasty dishes.

Leave the Peachy Almond Pizza in the kitchen until the table is cleared. It's so impressive you should show it off whole. Cut serving pieces at the table. After this presentation, you deserve a promotion! Serves 6 to 8 people.

MAKE-AHEAD PLAN:

- **Summer-Harvest Soup**—Make up to 24 hours ahead. Heat the soup and add sour cream and dill at the last minute.
- **Leeks Mimosa**—Make up to 24 hours ahead; marinate overnight.
- **Golden-Glow Bake**—Make up to 24 hours ahead. Refrigerate in a baking dish.
- **Herbed Chèvre-Cheese Bread**—Make up to 24 hours ahead. Refrigerate bread in foil. If oven is crowded, heat 1/2 loaf of bread at a time in a toaster oven.
- **Raspberry-Sauced Chicken Breasts**—Double recipe if guests are hearty meat-eaters. Prepare chicken up to 24 hours ahead. At serving time, heat sauce, very carefully adding butter.
- **Peachy Almond Pizza**—Make crust and filling up to 24 hours ahead; refrigerate. Add peach topping about 2 hours before serving.

Short-Cuts:

- Serve plain French bread instead of Herbed Chèvre-Cheese Bread.
- Substitute buttered carrots for Golden-Glow Bake.
- Use a pie-crust mix for crust of Peachy Almond Pizza.

Raspberry-Sauced Chicken Breasts   *Photo on page 62.*

A snappy chicken dish with lots of style.

8 chicken-breast halves
1/2 teaspoon salt
1/4 teaspoon pepper
2 tablespoons butter or margarine
2 tablespoons vegetable oil
1 (12-oz.) pkg. frozen unsweetened
    raspberries or 1 pint fresh raspberries
1/4 cup red wine

1 garlic clove, crushed
1 tablespoon minced parsley
1/2 cup chicken broth or bouillon
2 teaspoons green peppercorns,
    slightly crushed
1/4 cup butter, cut in 1/2-inch pieces
Enoki mushrooms, if desired

Sprinkle chicken with salt and pepper. Melt 2 tablespoons butter or margarine in a large skillet; add oil. Add seasoned chicken; brown on both sides. Mash 1/2 of raspberries; press through a fine sieve to remove seeds. Refrigerate remaining berries. In a small bowl, combine strained berries, wine, garlic, parsley and broth or bouillon. Pour over chicken. Cover skillet; cook 15 minutes over medium heat. *Complete now or make ahead.*

To complete now, cook chicken in sauce until tender. Using a slotted spoon, place hot chicken on a platter or serving dish; keep hot. Stir green peppercorns into sauce; remove from heat. Add 1/4 cup butter, 1 or 2 pieces at a time, stirring constantly until butter is blended into sauce. Immediately spoon over hot chicken; garnish with reserved raspberries and enoki mushrooms, if desired. Serve hot.

To make ahead, place cooked chicken and sauce in separate containers with a tight-fitting lids. Cool; refrigerate up to 24 hours. Reheat in a large skillet, adding batter as directed above. Garnish and serve as directed above. Makes 8 servings.

Summer-Harvest Soup

This flavor combination is so smooth your guests will never guess the ingredients.

4 bacon slices, chopped
1 small onion, chopped
4 yellow crookneck squash
2 cups fresh green peas or
    1 (10-oz.) pkg. frozen green peas
2 cups chicken broth or bouillon

1/2 teaspoon salt
1/8 teaspoon pepper
1 teaspoon Worcestershire sauce
1/2 cup dairy sour cream
1/2 teaspoon dried dill weed
Fresh dill sprigs

In a large saucepan, cook bacon and onion until onion is soft. Dice unpeeled squash. Add diced squash, green peas, broth or bouillon, salt, pepper and Worcestershire sauce to saucepan. Simmer until vegetables are tender, about 7 minutes. In a blender or food processor fitted with a metal blade, puree 1/2 of squash mixture at a time. *Complete now or make ahead.*

To complete now, return pureed mixture to saucepan; heat to boiling point. Remove from heat; stir in sour cream and dill weed. Serve in a soup tureen or in individual soup bowls. Garnish with dill sprigs.

To make ahead, cool; pour puree into a container with a tight-fitting lid. Refrigerate up to 24 hours. Reheat and serve as directed above. Makes 5 or 6 servings.

Impressing the V.I.P.

Surprise your V.I.P. with this unusual menu, featuring ever popular chicken breasts that are flavored with a wonderful peppery raspberry sauce.

Accent the meal with less-known vegetables such as enoki mushrooms and a colorful salad of Leeks Mimosa.

Clockwise from top: Herbed Chèvre-Cheese Bread, page 66, Golden-Glow Bake, page 65, Leeks Mimosa, page 66, and Raspberry-Sauced Chicken Breasts, page 61.

How to Make Peachy Almond Pizza

1/Cool baked cheesecake; refrigerate up to 24 hours. Arrange 4 cups peach slices over top.

2/Spoon glaze over peaches; garnish with peach-tree leaves and slivered almonds, if desired.

Golden-Glow Bake

Photo on pages 62-63.

A magical combination of flavors that will keep your guests fascinated.

6 medium boiling potatoes, peeled, cubed	1/4 teaspoon pepper
1 onion, coarsely chopped	1 egg, lightly beaten
6 medium carrots, peeled, cubed	1/2 cup half and half
1/4 cup butter or margarine, room temperature	1 tablespoon minced parsley
	2 tablespoons butter or margarine, melted
1 teaspoon salt	Minced parsley

In a medium saucepan, cook potatoes in lightly salted water until tender; drain. Press through a food mill or ricer into a large bowl. Or, in a large bowl, mash potatoes with a potato masher. In another medium saucepan, cook onion and carrots in lightly salted water until tender; drain. Puree cooked onion and carrots in a food processor fitted with a metal blade. Add to potato puree; stir in 1/4 cup butter or margarine, salt, pepper, egg, half and half and 1 tablespoon minced parsley. Spoon into a 1-1/2-quart baking dish. Make a rough texture on top of vegetables using a small metal spatula. *Complete now or make ahead.*

To complete now, drizzle 2 tablespoons melted butter over vegetable mixture. Place in cold oven. Turn oven to 350F (175C). Bake 25 to 35 minutes or until heated through and slightly browned on top. Garnish with minced parsley; serve hot.

To make ahead, cover with foil or plastic wrap; refrigerate up to 24 hours. Drizzle with melted butter; bake 35 to 45 minutes as directed above. Sprinkle with parsley. Makes 6 to 8 servings.

Peachy Almond Pizza

Finish dinner in high style with this stupendous fresh-peach dessert.

1/4 cup lightly packed brown sugar
3/4 cup all-purpose flour
1/4 cup butter or margarine,
   room temperature
1/4 cup finely chopped toasted almonds
1 (8-oz.) pkg. cream cheese,
   room temperature

1/4 cup granulated sugar
1 egg
1 tablespoon lemon juice
2 tablespoons milk
1/2 teaspoon vanilla extract
About 6 large ripe peaches
1 tablespoon lemon juice

Peach Glaze:
1 cup sliced peaches from peaches above
1/2 cup sugar
2 tablespoons cornstarch
3/4 cup water
1 tablespoon almond-flavored liqueur

1 or 2 drops red food coloring
Peach-tree leaves, if desired
2 tablespoons toasted slivered almonds,
   if desired

Preheat oven to 400F (205C). In a small bowl, combine brown sugar and flour. With a pastry blender or 2 knives, cut in butter or margarine until crumbly. Stir in almonds. Press over bottom of a 12-inch pizza pan. Bake in preheated oven 10 to 12 minutes or until golden brown. While crust bakes, in a medium bowl, beat cream cheese and granulated sugar until smooth. Beat in egg, 1 tablespoon lemon juice, milk and vanilla. Remove baked crust from oven; set aside. Reduce heat to 350F (175C). Pour cheese mixture over baked crust. Return to oven; bake 20 to 25 minutes or until firm. Cool completely on a rack. *Complete now or make ahead.*

To complete now, peel and slice peaches, making 5 cups sliced peaches. Place sliced peaches in a large bowl; sprinkle with 1 tablespoon lemon juice. Prepare Peach Glaze. Arrange remaining 4 cups peach slices over baked cheese mixture in a spiral. Spoon glaze over peaches. Garnish with peach-tree leaves and slivered almonds, if desired. Refrigerate at least 2 hours. To serve, cut into wedges.

To make Peach Glaze, puree 1 cup peach slices by mashing with a fork or processing in a blender or food processor fitted with a metal blade; set aside. In a small saucepan, combine sugar and cornstarch; stir in water until blended. Add pureed peaches. Stirring constantly, cook over medium heat until mixture thickens. Press through a strainer into a small bowl. Stir in liqueur and food coloring.

To make ahead, cover cooled pizza with foil or plastic wrap. Refrigerate up to 24 hours. Top with peach slices and glaze. Garnish as directed above. Makes 6 to 8 servings.

Leeks Mimosa

Photo on pages 62-63.

A colorful salad that's a slightly different flavor combination.

6 medium leeks, trimmed
2 cups beef broth or bouillon
1/3 cup tarragon vinegar
1 tablespoon chopped parsley
2 tablespoons sweet-pickle relish, drained
1 tablespoon chopped pimento
1/2 teaspoon salt

1/4 teaspoon pepper
1/4 teaspoon paprika
1/2 cup vegetable oil or olive oil
Lettuce leaves
2 hard-cooked eggs, chopped
6 cherry tomatoes, halved

Cut off and discard dark green tops, leaving leeks about 7 inches long. Cut each leek in half lengthwise, then lengthwise again. Wash thoroughly to remove sand; drain on paper towels. Place drained leek pieces in a large skillet. Add broth or bouillon; cover skillet. Cook 8 to 10 minutes or until tender. Drain and cool; place cooled leeks in a shallow bowl. In a small bowl, combine vinegar, parsley, pickle relish, pimento, salt, pepper, paprika and oil. Pour over cooled leeks. Cover bowl with foil or plastic wrap. *Complete now or make ahead.*

To complete now, refrigerate in marinade at least 2 hours. If olive oil is used, remove from refrigerator about 30 minutes before serving. To serve, drain off marinade. Arrange lettuce leaves on an oval platter or serving dish; place marinated leeks on lettuce leaves. Sprinkle with hard-cooked eggs. Garnish with cherry tomatoes; serve cold or at room temperature.

To make ahead, refrigerate in marinade up to 24 hours. Up to 3 hours before serving, drain off marinade; arrange on lettuce leaves. Refrigerate until served. If olive oil is used, remove from refrigerator about 30 minutes before serving. Garnish and serve as directed above. Makes 6 servings.

● ● ●

Herbed Chèvre-Cheese Bread

Photo on pages 62-63.

Goat cheese teams up with herbs for a wonderful flavor surprise.

1 (8-oz.) unsliced baguette French bread
4 to 5 oz. goat cheese, room temperature
1/2 cup butter or margarine,
    room temperature
1 teaspoon minced chives
1 tablespoon minced parsley

1/2 teaspoon Dijon-style mustard
1/4 teaspoon dried leaf thyme or
    3/4 teaspoon chopped thyme leaves
1/4 teaspoon dried dill weed or
    1 teaspoon chopped fresh dill

Cut bread in half lengthwise. Cut each half in crosswise slices, 1 inch apart, almost to bottom crust, leaving some of crust uncut. Set aside. Cut cheese into 1/2-inch cubes. In a food processor fitted with a metal blade or with an electric mixer, beat all ingredients except bread until blended, with small pieces of herbs showing. Keeping slices together, spread cheese mixture over cut side of each half of bread. Wrap each bread half airtight in foil. *Complete now or make ahead.*

To complete now, preheat oven to 400F (205C). Bake foil-wrapped bread 10 minutes or until hot. Cut slices apart; arrange slices in a serving bowl or on a platter.

To make ahead, refrigerate wrapped bread up to 24 hours. Bake and serve as directed above. Makes 6 to 8 servings.

Good Old Summertime Brunch

Mimosas
Zucchini-Cheese Wheel
Broiled Tomatoes
Jumbo Popovers   Fresh Plum Butter
Sunrise Fruit
Orange-Chocolate Logs

*S*et the stage for a bright and cheerful brunch on your patio or porch. Decorate with colorful pots or flats of flowering plants to create the atmosphere for a happy time. When guests arrive, offer them a sparkling Mimosa to sip while you're getting everything on the table. You don't need a recipe for the Mimosas—just pour chilled orange juice into each champagne glass until it's half full. Then fill it with chilled champagne; top with a thin slice of orange. Encourage everyone to bring their drinks to the table while you start serving warm wedges of Zucchini-Cheese Wheel and Broiled Tomatoes. Bring out Jumbo Popovers, piping hot from the oven. Pass Fresh Plum Butter for a slightly different spread to enhance the popovers.

After everyone has finished eating, clear the table and show off the Sunrise Fruit. Sparkling frosted grapes top off fresh nectarines and kiwifruit. Orange-Chocolate Logs provide a crunchy contrast in texture and flavor. Serves 6 people.

MAKE-AHEAD PLAN:

- **Orange-Chocolate Logs**—Make and freeze up to 1 month ahead.
- **Jumbo Popovers**—Make and freeze up to 7 days ahead. Reheat to serve. Or, pour batter into custard cups; refrigerate up to 1 hour before baking.
- **Zucchini-Cheese Wheel**—Make and freeze up to 5 days ahead. Or, make up to 24 hours ahead; refrigerate. Or, allow extra baking time for frozen version. If you have only 1 oven, bake early enough so it will be out of the oven about 1 hour before serving time. Cover with foil; keep on a hot tray while baking popovers.
- **Fresh Plum Butter**—Make up to 4 days ahead.
- **Broiled Tomatoes**—Make up to 24 hours ahead. Broil immediately before serving.
- **Mimosas**—Slice oranges early in the day; refrigerate in a plastic bag.
- **Sunrise Fruit**—Frost grapes up to 24 hours ahead; store at room temperature or in a cool place. Do not refrigerate. Prepare other fruit up to 3 hours before serving.

Short-Cuts:

- Purchase your favorite jam instead of making Fresh Plum Butter.
- Substitute bottled or reconstituted frozen orange juice for Mimosas.
- Purchase bakery muffins or a coffeecake instead of making Jumbo Popovers.

Jumbo Popovers

This batter contains an extra egg which insures larger and more impressive popovers.

3 eggs
1 cup milk
2 tablespoons butter or margarine, melted

1 cup all-purpose flour
1/4 teaspoon salt

Generously grease 6 (6-ounce) custard cups; set aside. In a medium bowl or in a blender, beat all ingredients until smooth. Pour into greased cups. *Complete now or make ahead.*

To complete now, preheat oven to 400F (205C) while preparing batter. Place filled custard cups in a jelly-roll pan. Bake in preheated oven 40 to 50 minutes or until surface is browned and center is moist but not gummy. Cut open 1 popover to test for doneness. Serve hot.

To make ahead, refrigerate batter in custard cups up to 1 hour. Place cups in a jelly-roll pan. Bake in preheated oven 50 to 60 minutes or until surface is browned and center is moist but not gummy; serve hot. If desired, freeze baked popovers up to 7 days. To reheat, return to clean custard cups. Preheat oven to 350F (175C); heat 8 to 10 minutes. Makes 6 servings.

• ● ● •

Fresh Plum Butter

Spread on muffins, popovers or toast.

4 ripe plums, pitted, chopped
1 cup powdered sugar

1 cup butter, room temperature

In a blender or food processor fitted with a metal blade, combine plums, powdered sugar and butter. Blend until smooth and creamy. *Complete now or make ahead.*

To complete now, spoon into a serving dish; refrigerate at least 15 minutes. Serve slightly chilled. Use leftovers on toast or muffins the next day.

To make ahead, spoon into a 3-cup container with a tight-fitting lid. Refrigerate up to 3 or 4 days, depending on ripeness of plums. Makes 2-1/2 to 3 cups.

• ● ● •

Broiled Tomatoes

A colorful vegetable accent.

3 medium tomatoes
1/2 cup soft bread crumbs
1/2 teaspoon dried leaf basil

1/4 teaspoon salt
1/8 teaspoon pepper
1 tablespoon butter

Cut tomatoes in half crosswise. Make 4 or 5 (1/4-inch-deep) slashes across cut-side of each tomato half. In a small bowl, combine bread crumbs, basil, salt and pepper. Sprinkle on cut-side of each tomato half. Dot each with butter. *Complete now or make ahead.*

To complete now, preheat broiler. Broil crumb-topped tomatoes, 5 to 6 inches from heat, until golden brown. Arrange on a platter or serving dish; serve hot.

To make ahead, cover with plastic wrap or foil; refrigerate up to 24 hours. Remove cover; broil and serve as directed above. Makes 6 servings.

Clockwise from top right: Orange Juice for Mimosas, page
67, Jumbo Popovers and Sunrise Fruit, page 71.

Good Old Summertime Brunch • 69

How to Make Zucchini-Cheese Wheel

1/Line bottom and side of pan with cooked zucchini, letting ends drape over outside of pan.

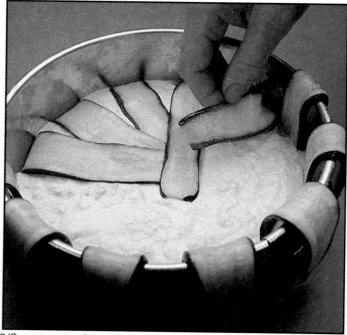

2/Spoon egg mixture into zucchini-lined pan. Fold zucchini ends over filling.

Zucchini-Cheese Wheel

It's the kind of dish you want to keep on eating.

3 medium zucchini
2 tablespoons vegetable oil
2 eggs
8 oz. cottage cheese (1 cup)
1/4 cup butter or margarine,
   room temperature
1/4 cup all-purpose flour

1/2 teaspoon baking powder
1/4 teaspoon salt
1/2 pint dairy sour cream (1 cup)
1 tablespoon minced green onion
3 slices boiled or baked ham, finely chopped
   (about 2 oz.)
1/4 cup grated Parmesan cheese (3/4 oz.)

Cut each zucchini into 6 lengthwise slices. Heat oil in a large skillet; add zucchini slices. Cook over medium heat only until softened but not cooked. Line bottom of an ungreased 8-inch springform pan with 6 slices cooked zucchini. Line side with remaining slices, letting ends drape over outside of pan; set aside. In a medium bowl, beat eggs with an electric mixer. Beat in cottage cheese and butter or margarine until almost smooth. In a small bowl, blend flour, baking powder and salt. Stir into egg mixture. Stir in sour cream, green onion, ham and Parmesan cheese. Spoon into zucchini-lined pan. Fold zucchini ends over filling toward center of pan. *Complete now or make ahead.*

To complete now, preheat oven to 350F (175C). Bake 40 to 50 minutes; cool on a wire rack 10 minutes. Remove side of springform pan. Cut wheel into wedges; serve warm or cold. To keep warm, cover with foil; place on a hot tray.

To make ahead, cover with foil; refrigerate up to 24 hours or freeze up to 5 days. Bake early enough before brunch to leave at least 1 hour to bake popovers. To bake refrigerated version, preheat oven to 350F (175C). Remove cover; bake 40 to 50 minutes or until lightly browned. For frozen version, thaw at room temperature 30 minutes; then bake, uncovered, in preheated oven 45 to 55 minutes until lightly browned. Serve as directed above. Makes about 6 servings.

Sunrise Fruit   *Photo on page 68.*

Frosted grapes add a touch of glamour to these refreshing fruits.

1 egg white
1 tablespoon water
1/4 cup sugar
6 to 8 small clusters red seedless grapes

3 ripe nectarines
2 ripe kiwifruit
1 tablespoon minced crystallized ginger,
   if desired

In a small bowl, combine egg white and water; beat gently until blended but not frothy. Pour sugar into another small bowl. Dip 1 small cluster of grapes into egg-white mixture; then coat with sugar. Place on a large plate. Repeat until all grapes are coated. *Complete now or make ahead.*

To complete now, slice nectarines; peel and slice kiwifruit. Arrange nectarine and kiwifruit slices on a glass platter or in individual sherbet glasses. Sprinkle with crystallized ginger, if desired. Garnish with clusters of frosted grapes. Serve immediately.

To make ahead, store frosted grapes at room temperature up to 24 hours. Slice nectarines 2 to 3 hours before serving. Serve as directed above. Makes 6 to 8 servings.

Orange-Chocolate Logs

Crispy, crunchy and a guaranteed hit!

1/4 cup butter
1/2 cup granulated sugar
2 teaspoons grated orange peel
1 oz. semisweet chocolate, grated

2 egg whites
1/2 cup all-purpose flour
Powdered sugar

Preheat oven to 325F (165C). In a large bowl, beat butter and granulated sugar until light and fluffy. Stir in orange peel and chocolate. In a small bowl, beat egg whites until stiff but not dry. Fold into chocolate mixture alternately with flour. Drop batter by heaping teaspoons, about 3 inches apart, on an ungreased baking sheet. Dip the back of a spoon in cold water. Use to flatten each mound of batter to a 3-inch circle. Bake in preheated oven 10 minutes. Working quickly while cookies are still warm, roll cookie around handle of a wooden spoon. Gently remove from wooden-spoon handle. If cookies becomes too stiff to roll, return to oven for a few minutes. Cool, seam-side down, on a wire rack. *Complete now or make ahead.*

To complete now, sprinkle cooled logs with powdered sugar; arrange on a serving plate. Serve immediately.

To make ahead, arrange cooled rolled cookies in a single layer in a container with firm sides and a tight-fitting lid. Freeze up to 1 month. Thaw at room temperature. Serve as directed above. Makes about 20 logs.

After-Tennis Brunch

Grapefruit Cardinale
Hearty Brunch Soufflé
Herbed English Muffins
Fennel Salad
Asparagus in Browned Butter
Touch-of-Gold Cookies

*I*nvite your tennis buddies back to your house for brunch after the morning game. They'll think you're a winner in the kitchen as well as on the tennis court. Everything is made ahead, except for minor last-minute details. Cook about 2 pounds fresh asparagus up to 24 hours ahead. Set the table before you leave for tennis. Take the Hearty Brunch Soufflé out of refrigerator if you won't be away longer than an hour.

As soon as you return home, put the soufflé in the oven to heat. This is not a true soufflé that falls as soon as it's taken out of the oven. It will hold its shape beautifully. If at room temperature, it will heat in the oven in less than 30 minutes. While the soufflé cooks, melt about 1/4 cup butter. When the butter is a golden color, add the cooked asparagus. Sprinkle with a little salt and pepper. Mound grapefruit sections and berries in the grapefruit shells; serve them while the soufflé heats. Just before the soufflé is ready, toast six English muffins. Your friends will want more of these herb-flavored muffins, so toast more as they're needed. Serves 6 people.

MAKE-AHEAD PLAN:

- **Touch-of-Gold Cookies**—Make and freeze up to 1 month ahead.
- **Herbed English Muffins**—Make and freeze up to 1 month ahead. Or, make 2 days ahead and store at room temperature. Toast and butter muffins at the last minute.
- **Fennel Salad**—Make up to 24 hours ahead; drain at serving time.
- **Grapefruit Cardinale**—Up to 24 hours ahead, cut grapefruit and prepare sauce. Put together minutes before serving.
- **Asparagus in Browned Butter**—Cook asparagus up to 24 hours ahead; heat in butter at serving time.
- **Hearty Brunch Soufflé**—Make up to 24 hours ahead. Bake about 40 minutes before serving.

Short-Cuts:

- Purchase English muffins.
- Serve plain grapefruit.

Herbed English Muffins

These made-from-scratch muffins are enhanced by an interesting combination of herbs.

1 (1/4-oz.) pkg. active dry yeast
   (1 tablespoon)
1 cup warm water (110F, 45C)
3 tablespoons sugar
1 teaspoon salt
2 tablespoons butter or margarine,
   room temperature

1 cup milk, room temperature
1/2 teaspoon dried dill weed
1/2 teaspoon celery salt
1/4 teaspoon ground sage
5 to 5-1/2 cups all-purpose flour
Cornmeal
Butter or margarine

In a large bowl, sprinkle yeast over water. Let stand until yeast is softened. Stir in sugar, salt, 2 tablespoons butter or margarine, milk, dill weed, celery salt, sage and 2 cups flour. Beat until smooth. Stir in enough remaining flour to make a stiff dough. On a lightly floured surface, knead 2 minutes or until dough can be shaped into a ball. Clean and grease bowl. Place dough in bowl, turning to grease all sides. Cover; let rise in a warm place, free from drafts, 1 hour or until doubled in bulk. Sprinkle cornmeal over 2 ungreased baking sheets; set aside. Punch down dough; divide in half. Roll out each half until 1/2 inch thick. Using a round 3- or 3-1/2-inch cutter, cut dough into rounds. Place muffins, 2 inches apart, on prepared baking sheets. Cover; let rise 30 minutes or until doubled in bulk. Place a griddle over medium heat. When hot, lightly grease griddle. With a spatula, place muffin, cornmeal-side down, on hot griddle. Cook over medium-low heat, or at 300F (150C) on an electric griddle, 6 to 8 minutes on each side. Cool completely on a rack. *Complete now or make ahead.*

To complete now, use a sharp knife to cut muffins in half. Toast; spread with butter or margarine.

To make ahead, place cooled muffins in a plastic bag; seal. Store 1 to 2 days at room temperature. To store longer, place in freezer bags; seal. Freeze up to 1 month. Thaw in refrigerator. Serve as directed above. Makes 14 to 16 muffins.

Grapefruit Cardinale

Beautiful red color and delicious to eat!

3 grapefruit
1 (10-oz.) pkg. frozen raspberries or
   strawberries in sugar syrup, thawed

2 tablespoons raspberry-flavored liqueur

Cut grapefruit in half crosswise. Using a small sharp knife, cut on each side of membranes separating fruit sections. Cut around outside of sections to separate from shell; do not cut through shell. Use a spoon to scoop out fruit sections. With scissors, cut center membrane. Remove all membranes from grapefruit halves, leaving shells intact; set shells aside. In a medium bowl, combine thawed berries, liqueur and grapefruit sections. *Complete now or make ahead.*

To complete now, spoon grapefruit-berry mixture into reserved grapefruit shells. Serve cold.

To make ahead, cover and refrigerate grapefruit-berry mixture up to 24 hours. Place grapefruit shells in a plastic bag; refrigerate separately. Serve as directed above. Makes 6 servings.

Hearty Brunch Soufflé

Meal-in-a-dish that appeals to hearty brunch appetites.

8 eggs
2 tablespoons water
2 tablespoons butter or margarine
1 lb. bulk pork sausage
2 tablespoons vegetable oil
1 lb. frozen, loosely packed,
   hash-brown potatoes

1-1/2 cups dairy sour cream
1/3 cup minced green onions
1 cup shredded Cheddar cheese (4 oz.)
1 tomato, cut into thin wedges

Grease a 2-quart baking dish or soufflé dish; set aside. In a medium bowl, lightly beat eggs and water until blended. Melt butter or margarine in a 10-inch skillet; pour in egg mixture. Without stirring, cook over medium heat. As eggs set, lift up edge with a spatula, letting uncooked eggs flow underneath. When eggs are softly set, gently slide onto a cutting board; cool to room temperature. Cut into 2″ x 1/2″ strips; set aside. Crumble sausage into a large skillet. Cook over medium heat until browned and no longer pink, using a fork to stir and break up sausage. Drain, discarding drippings. Remove browned sausage; set aside. In same skillet, heat oil; add potatoes. Stirring occasionally, cook over medium heat until golden brown. Spread browned potatoes in bottom of greased dish. Spread 1/2 of sour cream over potatoes. Layering each in turn, top with all of green onions, all of cooked sausage, all of cooked egg strips and remaining sour cream. Sprinkle cheese over top. *Complete now or make ahead.*

To complete now, place casserole in cold oven. Turn oven to 350F (175C). Bake 30 to 40 minutes or until cheese melts and mixture bubbles. Garnish with tomato wedges; serve hot.

To make ahead, cover with foil or plastic wrap; refrigerate up to 24 hours. Bake and serve as directed above. Makes 6 to 8 servings.

● ● ●

Fennel Salad

Expand your food horizon with this unusual salad combo.

3 cups thinly sliced fennel
1 small red onion, thinly sliced
3 tablespoons red-wine vinegar
1 tablespoon lemon juice
1 teaspoon Dijon-style mustard
1/2 teaspoon salt

1/4 teaspoon pepper
2 tablespoons minced watercress leaves
1/2 cup olive oil or vegetable oil
Lettuce
1 tablespoon chopped pimento

In a medium bowl, combine fennel and onion. In a small bowl, combine vinegar, lemon juice, mustard, salt, pepper, watercress and oil. Pour over fennel mixture; toss lightly. Cover with foil or plastic wrap. *Complete now or make ahead.*

To complete now, refrigerate at least 2 hours. To serve, drain vegetables. Line a shallow serving dish with lettuce. Spoon drained vegetables into lettuce-lined dish. Sprinkle with pimento; serve cold.

To make ahead, refrigerate up to 24 hours. Serve as directed above. Makes about 6 servings.

How to Make Hearty Brunch Soufflé

1/Over potatoes and 1/2 of sour cream, layer green onions, sausage, egg strips and remaining sour cream.

2/Sprinkle cheese over top. Bake until cheese melts and mixture bubbles. Garnish with tomato wedges.

Touch-of-Gold Cookies

Shredded carrots give a special flavor that your guests won't recognize.

1 cup vegetable shortening
3/4 cup sugar
2 eggs
2 cups all-purpose flour

2 teaspoons baking powder
1/2 teaspoon salt
1 cup grated carrots (about 3 medium)
1/3 cup chopped walnuts

Orange Frosting:
1-1/2 cups sifted powdered sugar
1 tablespoon orange juice

2 tablespoons butter or margarine,
   room temperature

Preheat oven to 375F (190C). In a large bowl, cream shortening; gradually beat in sugar. Add eggs; beat until smooth. In a small bowl, combine flour, baking powder and salt. Add to egg mixture; beat until smooth. Stir in carrots and walnuts. Drop dough by heaping teaspoons, 2 inches apart, on ungreased baking sheets. Bake in preheated oven 10 to 12 minutes or until golden brown. Remove from baking sheets; cool on wire racks. *Complete now or make ahead.*

To complete now, prepare frosting. Spread frosting over tops of cooled cookies.

To make Orange Frosting, in a small bowl, combine powdered sugar, orange juice and butter or margarine; beat with an electric mixer until fluffy.

To make ahead, wrap cookies airtight in freezer wrap. Freeze up to 1 month. Thaw at room temperature. Frost thawed cookies. Makes 50 to 55 cookies.

Tailgate Get-Together

Milanese Appetizer Cups
Golden-Harvest Soup
Buttered French Bread
Sportsmen's Special
Mixed Green Salad
Orange-Apricot Bars

*I*f you ask a sports fan to choose his favorite place for a dinner, he's likely to name the parking lot of his local stadium. Tailgating, or the custom of socializing with friends before the big game, received this name because the tailgate of a station wagon was used as a substitute for a serving table. Today, you don't need a station wagon to participate. Take along a folding table and chairs. Start off with our wonderful Milanese Appetizer Cups—everyone loves them hot or cold. Heat Golden-Harvest Soup just before leaving home; transport it in a large thermos. Your friends will enjoy drinking it out of coffee mugs.

Take Sportsmen's Special out of the oven, piping hot, just before you leave the house. Cover it with foil; then wrap it in 5 or 6 layers of newspaper and it will stay hot for about an hour. To serve it hot at a later time, bake Sportsmen's Special in a metal pan. Take along a hibachi to heat it. Tear the salad greens and transport them in a large bowl with a tight-fitting lid. Take along a favorite dressing to add before serving. Pass sliced French bread with the soup or salad. Just before the game starts, finish your meal with Orange-Apricot Bars. Serves 6 people.

MAKE-AHEAD PLAN:

- **Orange-Apricot Bars**—Make and freeze up to 2 months ahead.
- **Golden-Harvest Soup**—Make up to 24 hours ahead.
- **Sportsmen's Special**—Make up to 24 hours ahead. Allow about 1 hour to bake at serving time.
- **Milanese Appetizer Cups**—Make up to 24 hours ahead.

Short-Cuts:

- Serve Melba toast instead of French bread.
- Purchase small quiches; substitute for Milanese Appetizer Cups.

How to Make Milanese Appetizer Cups

1/Line miniature muffin cups with prosciutto. Spoon filling into lined cups.

2/Garnish each cold or hot appetizer with a dollop of sour cream and chopped green onions.

Milanese Appetizer Cups

Use miniature muffin pans for intriguing, individual appetizers.

1 (10-oz.) pkg. frozen chopped spinach	1/4 teaspoon salt
8 oz. ricotta cheese (1 cup)	1 egg, lightly beaten
1/2 cup grated Parmesan cheese (1-1/2 oz.)	24 thin slices prosciutto,
1 cup chopped mushrooms (about 3 oz.)	about 2 inches square
2 tablespoons minced onion	Dairy sour cream, if desired
1/4 teaspoon dried leaf oregano	2 green onions, if desired, thinly sliced

Cook spinach according to package directions. Pour cooked spinach into a sieve; drain thoroughly by gently pressing out excess juices with back of a spoon. In a medium bowl, combine drained spinach, ricotta cheese, Parmesan cheese, mushrooms, minced onion, oregano, salt and egg. Preheat oven to 375F (190C). Lightly butter 24 (1-3/4-inch) muffin cups. Place 1 slice prosciutto in each cup; press against bottom and side of cup. Spoon cheese mixture into prosciutto-lined cups. Bake in preheated oven 20 to 25 minutes. *Complete now or make ahead.*

To complete now, let stand 5 minutes. Gently run a knife around side of each cup to loosen appetizers; remove from cups. Serve hot or cold. If desired, garnish each appetizer with a dollop of sour cream and 2 or 3 green-onion slices.

To make ahead, cool in pan at room temperature 10 minutes. Cover with foil or plastic wrap; refrigerate up to 24 hours. To serve hot, preheat oven to 350F (175C). Remove cover; heat in muffin cups 6 to 10 minutes. Cool in pan 5 minutes; then gently loosen and remove from muffin cups. Garnish as directed above, if desired. Makes 24 appetizers.

Golden-Harvest Soup

An excellent "starter" for a memorable meal.

2 lbs. banana squash or hubbard squash
1 pint dairy sour cream (2 cups)
2 cooking apples, peeled, cored, cubed
1/2 teaspoon ground nutmeg
Salt and pepper to taste

2 tablespoons chopped onion
1/4 cup butter or margarine
1/4 cup all-purpose flour
1 qt. chicken broth or bouillon (4 cups)
4 bacon slices, cooked crisp, crumbled

Place squash, skin-side down, in a 13" x 9" baking pan; cover with foil. Place pan in oven; turn oven to 425F (220C). Bake 60 minutes or until tender. Remove skin; cut pulp into 1-inch cubes. In a blender or food processor fitted with a metal blade, process sour cream, apple, nutmeg, salt, pepper, onion and 1/2 of squash until smooth. Pour into a large bowl; puree remaining squash. In a large skillet or saucepan, melt butter or margarine. Stir in flour; stirring constantly, cook about 2 minutes. Gradually stir in chicken broth or bouillon. Cook, stirring constantly, until sauce is slightly thickened. Stir in pureed ingredients. *Complete now or make ahead.*

To complete now, heat combined mixtures almost to a boil; do not boil. Pour into a large thermos for transporting. Serve in soup bowls or mugs; sprinkle with bacon.

To make ahead, cool; cover and refrigerate up to 24 hours. Reheat squash mixture in a large saucepan. Serve as directed above. Makes about 8 servings.

Sportsman's Special

Creamy, delicious and spiced just right.

2 tablespoons vegetable oil
3 medium zucchini, sliced
1 medium onion, sliced
1 lb. lean ground beef
1/2 lb. mild Italian sausage
1/4 teaspoon dried leaf oregano
1 garlic clove, crushed
1/8 teaspoon ground cloves
Salt and pepper to taste

1 (6-oz.) can tomato paste
1/2 cup dry red wine
1/3 cup butter or margarine
1/3 cup all-purpose flour
1 pint half and half (2 cups)
1 cup chicken broth or bouillon
1/4 teaspoon salt
1/8 teaspoon ground nutmeg
1/4 cup grated Parmesan cheese (3/4 oz.)

Heat oil in a large skillet. Add zucchini and onion; sauté until vegetables are almost tender. Drain on paper towels. In same skillet, brown ground beef and sausage; discard drippings. Stir in oregano, garlic, cloves, salt, pepper, tomato paste and wine. Simmer 5 minutes; remove from heat. In a small heavy saucepan, melt butter or margarine. Stir in flour; stirring, cook 2 minutes. Stir in half and half, broth or bouillon, 1/4 teaspoon salt and nutmeg. Cook over medium heat, stirring, until mixture thickens; remove from heat. Spread drained zucchini and onion evenly in an ungreased 13" x 9" baking dish. Sprinkle with cheese. Spread meat mixture over cheese; then top with sauce. *Complete now or make ahead.*

To complete now, place layered casserole in cold oven. Turn oven to 350F (175C); bake 35 to 45 minutes or until bubbly. To transport, immediately cover tightly with foil. Wrap completely with 5 or 6 layers of newspaper to keep hot. To serve, spoon onto individual plates.

To make ahead, cover with foil; refrigerate up to 24 hours. About 1 hour before serving, remove foil. Bake in 350F (175C) oven 45 to 55 minutes. Let stand 5 minutes. Makes 6 servings.

How to Make Orange-Apricot Bars

1/Use a pastry blender or 2 knives to cut in butter.

2/Spread apricot mixture over half of crumbs, covering completely.

Orange-Apricot Bars

Popular for lunch boxes and picnics.

2 cups chopped dried apricots
1 orange, peeled, seeded, finely chopped
1-1/2 cups water
1/2 cup granulated sugar
1/2 cup chopped blanched almonds, toasted
2 cups all-purpose flour
2 cups quick-cooking rolled oats

3/4 cup lightly packed brown sugar
1 cup butter or margarine
1 tablespoon butter or margarine, melted
1 cup powdered sugar
1 to 1-1/2 tablespoons lemon juice or
orange juice

In a medium saucepan, combine apricots, orange, water and granulated sugar. Stirring, simmer 15 minutes or until thickened. Stir in almonds; set aside. Preheat oven to 375F (190C). Grease a 13" x 9" baking pan. In a medium bowl, combine flour, rolled oats and brown sugar. Cut in 1 cup butter or margarine with a pastry blender or 2 knives until mixture resembles coarse crumbs. Pat 1/2 of oats mixture over bottom of greased pan. Spread apricot mixture over crumbs. Top with remaining 1/2 of crumbs; pat gently. Bake in preheated oven 30 minutes. Cool in pan on a wire rack. In a small bowl, combine 1 tablespoon butter or margarine, powdered sugar and enough juice to make a smooth glaze. Drizzle over cooled mixture. After glaze sets, cut into bars. *Complete now or make ahead.*

To complete now, place glazed bars in a container with a tight-fitting lid for transporting.

To make ahead, place glazed bars in a container with a tight-fitting lid; store at room temperature up to 24 hours. Or, wrap in freezer wrap; freeze up to 2 months. Thaw at room temperature. Makes 32 to 40 bars.

Reunion of School Friends

New-Potato Appetizers
Taste-of-the-Orient Meatballs
Vegetable-Cutout Appetizers
Monsoon Pork Satay
Northern-Lights Cheese Ball
Mini Almond Cakes
Chocolate-Hazelnut Meringue Cookies
Wine   Beer   Soft Drinks

How exciting it is to get together with your favorite buddies from school! So that no one will miss any of the conversation, set up a buffet table of make-ahead finger foods. Guests can pick up bite-size morsels while catching up on the news. Provide small plates and cocktail napkins for handling these finger foods.

Plan on one or two hot foods. Bring them out once during the evening or keep them warm in chafing dishes or on hot trays. Include individual servings of desserts that are easy to pick up and eat.

In another area, set up beer, wine and soft drinks on a bar, table or serving cart. Keep beverages cold in ice chests. Let guests help themselves.

This menu is also ideal for a small reception. Serves 20 to 25 people.

MAKE-AHEAD PLAN:

- **Mini Almond Cakes**—Make and freeze up to 1 month ahead. Or, store in an airtight container up to 7 days at room temperature.
- **Chocolate-Hazelnut Meringue Cookies**—Bake and freeze up to 1 month ahead. Or, bake up to 24 hours ahead.
- **Taste-of-the-Orient Meatballs**—Make and freeze meatballs up to 3 weeks ahead. Thaw frozen meatballs overnight in the refrigerator. Or, make up to 24 hours ahead; refrigerate.
- **Northern-Lights Cheese Ball**—Make up to 24 hours ahead.
- **Monsoon Pork Satay**—Make up to 24 hours ahead. Broil just before serving.
- **New-Potato Appetizer**—Cook potatoes and fill up to 24 hours ahead. Broil before serving.
- **Vegetable-Cutout Appetizers**—Make up to 2 hours ahead.

Short-Cuts:

- Delete 1 or 2 items from menu.
- Serve wedges or slices of gjetost cheese and Jarlsberg cheese instead of cheese ball.

Monsoon Pork Satay

A mouthwatering way to start a party!

1/4 cup soy sauce
1/4 cup dry white wine
2 tablespoons brown sugar
1 garlic clove, crushed

Dipping Sauce:
1/2 cup chunk-style peanut butter
1/2 teaspoon crushed dried red pepper
1/2 teaspoon ground ginger
2 tablespoons honey

1/2 cup vegetable oil
1 lb. boneless pork or boneless chicken
  breast, cut in 1-inch cubes

1 tablespoon lemon juice
1 green onion, chopped
1 tablespoon dry white wine

In a 9" x 5" loaf pan, combine soy sauce, wine, brown sugar, garlic and oil. Add pork or chicken; spoon marinade over meat. Cover with foil or plastic wrap. *Complete now or make ahead.*

To complete now, marinate meat in refrigerator at least 4 hours. While meat marinates, prepare Dipping Sauce. Preheat broiler. Drain marinade from meat; discard marinade. Place marinated meat cubes on a broiler pan. Broil meat about 6 inches from heat until all sides are browned. Arrange broiled meat on a platter or serving plate. Insert a wooden pick into each meat cube. Serve with sauce.

To make Dipping Sauce, in a blender or food processor fitted with a metal blade, combine all sauce ingredients. Process until almost smooth.

To make ahead, refrigerate meat in marinade up to 24 hours. Broil and serve meat as directed above. Makes about 60 meat cubes or about 20 appetizer servings.

● ● ●

Vegetable-Cutout Appetizers

Vegetable hearts, flowers, stars, bells or animals give a festive look to your appetizer tray.

2 medium turnips
1 jicama (about 2 lbs.)
2 cups shredded sharp Cheddar cheese
  (8 oz.)
1/4 cup mayonnaise
1 teaspoon Dijon-style mustard

1/8 teaspoon paprika
1/2 teaspoon Worcestershire sauce
1/4 teaspoon salt
Pimento-stuffed green olives, sliced
Watercress
Pimento strips

Cut turnips and jicama crosswise into 1/4-inch slices. Use small cookie cutters, 1-1/2 to 2 inches in diameter, to make seasonal cutout designs. Save trimmings of vegetables for salad or soup. In a food processor fitted with a metal blade, process cheese, mayonnaise, mustard, paprika, Worcestershire sauce and salt until blended. Spoon into a pastry bag fitted with large star tip. Pipe a swirl of cheese mixture onto each vegetable cutout. Top each with an olive slice, watercress sprig or pimento strip. *Complete now or make ahead.*

To complete now, arrange appetizers on a platter or serving plate; serve immediately.

To make ahead, place appetizers on baking sheets or in shallow baking pans. Lightly cover with foil or plastic wrap; refrigerate up to 2 hours. Serve as directed above. Makes about 16 turnip and 46 jicama appetizers.

How to Make New-Potato Appetizers

1/With a melon baller or small spoon, scoop out centers, leaving a 1/4-inch shell.

2/Sprinkle cheese or caviar over sour-cream mixture. Broil only those topped with cheese.

New-Potato Appetizer

Use the very smallest potatoes for bite-size treats.

1-1/2 lbs. small new potatoes (about 20)
1/2 pint dairy sour cream (1 cup)
4 bacon slices, cooked crisp, crumbled
1/2 teaspoon seasoned salt
1/4 teaspoon pepper

2 teaspoons minced chives
1/2 cup shredded Cheddar cheese (2 oz.) or
grated Parmesan cheese (1-1/2 oz.)
Minced parsley

Cook whole unpeeled potatoes in boiling water until fork tender but not mushy. Place in cold water to stop cooking; cut each cooked potato in half. With a melon baller or small spoon, scoop out centers, leaving a 1/4-inch shell of pulp in skins. Use centers for soups or salads. In a small bowl, combine sour cream, bacon, seasoned salt, pepper and chives. Spoon sour-cream mixture evenly into centers of cooked potatoes. Sprinkle tops with cheese. Arrange on a baking sheet. *Complete now or make ahead.*

To complete now, preheat broiler. Place stuffed potatoes under broiler until cheese melts. Arrange broiled appetizers on a platter or serving plate. Garnish with parsley.

To make ahead, cover with foil or plastic wrap; refrigerate up to 24 hours. Broil and garnish as directed above. Makes about 40 appetizers.

Variation
Omit bacon. Top scooped-out potatoes with sour-cream mixture. When ready to serve, spoon a little golden caviar on top of each. Do not broil. Garnish with minced parsley or fresh dill.

Northern-Lights Cheese Ball

Photo on page 80.

Wonderful caramel-like flavor of Norwegian cheese makes this treat special.

2 cups shredded gjetost cheese (8 oz.)
2 (3-oz.) pkgs. cream cheese, well chilled
2 tablespoon fruit chutney, finely chopped
1 teaspoon minced fresh chives
1/4 teaspoon ground ginger

1/2 cup finely chopped walnuts
Norwegian flatbread
2 to 4 apples, cored, thinly sliced
2 to 4 pears, cored, thinly sliced

In a medium bowl, combine gjetost cheese, cream cheese, chutney, chives and ginger. With a pastry blender, blend ingredients until well mixed, but still mottled in color. Working on a firm, flat surface, shape cheese mixture into a ball. Flatten ball until about 2 inches thick. Press chopped walnuts onto outside of cheese. Wrap with plastic wrap. *Complete now or make ahead.*

To complete now, refrigerate at least 2 hours. To serve, unwrap cheese ball; place on a medium platter or serving plate. Surround with flatbread, apples and pears.

To make ahead, refrigerate 4 to 5 hours or overnight. Makes 1 cheese ball

● ● ●

Taste-of-the-Orient Meatballs

Unexpected crunchy texture, thanks to water chestnuts.

1/2 lb. uncooked shrimp, shelled,
   deveined, chopped
1/2 lb. uncooked lean pork, chopped
1/2 cup chopped celery stalks and leaves
1/4 cup chopped green onions
1 (8-oz.) can water chestnuts, drained

2 eggs, lightly beaten
1 tablespoon soy sauce
1/4 cup soft bread crumbs
1/2 teaspoon salt
1/4 teaspoon pepper

Dipping Sauce:
1/2 cup plain yogurt
1/2 cup fruit chutney, finely chopped
1/2 teaspoon curry powder

1/4 cup dry white wine
1/4 teaspoon grated gingerroot

Preheat oven to 375F (190C). In a food processor fitted with a metal blade, combine shrimp, pork, celery, green onions and water chestnuts. Process until finely chopped but not pureed. In a large bowl, combine eggs, soy sauce, bread crumbs, salt, pepper and meat mixture. Shape mixture into 36 (1-inch) balls. Arrange on a rack in a broiler pan. Bake in preheated oven 18 to 20 minutes or until golden brown. Drain; discard drippings. *Complete now or make ahead.*

To complete now, prepare Dipping Sauce. Keep meatballs warm in a chafing dish or on a hot tray. Serve with Dipping Sauce. Provide small wooden picks for meatballs.

To make Dipping Sauce, in a small bowl, combine all sauce ingredients.

To make ahead, cool; place meatballs in a container with a tight-fitting lid. Refrigerate up to 24 hours. Or, freeze individually on a baking sheet. Place in freezer bags; seal and keep frozen up to 3 weeks. Make and refrigerate Dipping Sauce up to 24 hours ahead. Thaw frozen meatballs in refrigerator overnight. To reheat, arrange refrigerated or thawed meatballs in a jelly-roll pan; cover with foil. Place in cold oven. Turn oven to 350F (175C). Heat 15 minutes or until warmed. Serve as directed above. Makes 36 meatballs and 1-1/4 cups sauce.

Mini Almond Cakes

If almond flavor is your weakness, these miniature cakes are for you.

1/2 teaspoon baking powder
1/2 cup all-purpose flour
1/2 cup butter, room temperature
1 (7- or 8-oz.) pkg. almond paste,
    room temperature

3/4 cup sugar
3 eggs
1 teaspoon grated orange peel
2/3 cup sliced almonds

Place miniature paper bon-bon cups in about 60 (1-3/4-inch) muffin cups. Preheat oven to 350F (175C). In a small bowl, combine baking powder and flour; set aside. In a large bowl, beat butter and almond paste until creamy. Add sugar; beat until light and fluffy. Add eggs, 1 at a time, beating well after each addition. Beat reserved flour mixture into egg mixture until smooth; stir in orange peel. Spoon about 1 teaspoon almond-paste mixture into each bon-bon cup. Sprinkle with sliced almonds. Bake in preheated oven 15 to 20 minutes or until golden brown. Bake in 2 to 3 batches, if necessary. *Complete now or make ahead.*

To complete now, cool about 5 minutes on a rack. Remove from muffin pans; arrange on a serving plate. Serve warm, or cool to room temperature before serving.

To make ahead, place on a rack; cool to room temperature. Remove from muffin cups; place in a container with a tight-fitting lid. Store up to 1 week at room temperature. Or, arrange in a single layer on baking sheets; freeze. Place frozen cakes in freezer bags. Seal bags; store in freezer up to 1 month. Thaw frozen cakes at room temperature at least 1 hour before serving as directed above. Makes about 60 mini-cakes.

●●●

Chocolate-Hazelnut Meringue Cookies

A perfect combination—slightly crunchy outside and a bit chewy inside.

1/3 cup finely ground blanched hazelnuts
1 tablespoon unsweetened cocoa powder
1/4 cup cornstarch
1/4 cup sugar

3 egg whites, room temperature
1/8 teaspoon cream of tartar
1/2 teaspoon vanilla extract
1/3 cup sugar

Grease a large baking sheet; set aside. Preheat oven to 325F (165C). In a small bowl, combine ground hazelnuts, cocoa powder, cornstarch and 1/4 cup sugar; set aside. In a large bowl, beat egg whites, cream of tartar and vanilla until foamy. Gradually beat in 1/3 cup sugar until stiff peaks form. Fold cocoa mixture into beaten egg-white mixture. Drop by teaspoons, about 1 inch apart, on greased baking sheet, making a curl on top with back of spoon. Bake in preheated oven 20 to 25 minutes or until tips begin to brown slightly. Let stand 5 minutes. With a metal spatula, remove from baking sheet; cool completely on a wire rack. *Complete now or make ahead.*

To complete now, arrange cooled cookies on a platter or serving plate. Serve immediately.

To make ahead, place cooled cookies in a single layer, in a rigid container with a tight-fitting lid. Store up to 1 week at room temperature. Or, return to baking sheet; freeze. Place in a rigid container with a tight-fitting lid; freeze up to 1 month. Serve as directed above. Makes about 40 cookies.

After a Day in the Snow

Chinese Walnuts   Popcorn
Hot Buttered Cider
Hearty Three-Bean Stew
Dilly Cheese Slices
Old-Fashioned Orange Sponge Cake

You and your friends have weathered the rigors of driving to the nearest winter resort for the week-end! After a day in the snow, whether you've been building snowmen or riding the ski lift, you're ready for hot and hearty food. Get out the Chinese Walnuts and Popcorn to munch on while the Hot Buttered Cider is heating. Then sit by the fire and thaw out while you enjoy this welcome drink. The Hearty Three-Bean Stew is really a meal-in-a-pot that takes about 15 minutes to heat. Dilly Cheese Slices offer a perfect complement to the stew and may be popped into the oven while still frozen. They're so good you'll need the whole batch for 8 people.

Old-Fashioned Orange Sponge Cake is easy to transport and just the right light finale to a stick-to-the-ribs meal. Serves 6 to 8 people.

MAKE-AHEAD PLAN:

- **Old-Fashioned Orange Sponge Cake**—Make and freeze up to 2 months ahead. Thaw at room temperature.
- **Chinese Walnuts**—Make up to 2 weeks ahead.
- **Dilly Cheese Slices**—Make and freeze up to 7 days ahead. If thawed before transporting, arrange in a single layer on baking sheets so they won't stick together.
- **Hot Buttered Cider**—Make 3 or 4 days ahead; reheat at serving time.
- **Hearty Three-Bean Stew**—Make up to 24 hours ahead. Transport in its cooking pan. Add beans and sausage; heat at serving time. Or, transfer to a slow-cooker; let heat while you play in the snow.

Short-Cuts:

- Substitute plain mixed nuts for Chinese Walnuts.
- Purchase a similar cake at a local bakery.
- Purchase a loaf of bread at a local bakery.

How to Make Dilly Cheese Slices

1/Dip bread slices into hot cheese mixture, coating completely. Let excess drain off.

2/Wrap frozen slices individually. Place in a freezer bag; store up to 7 days in freezer.

Dilly Cheese Slices

A bit more substantial than regular cheese bread.

1 (16-oz.) loaf French bread, unsliced
1/4 cup butter
5 cups shredded Cheddar cheese (1-1/4 lbs.)
2 teaspoons dried dill weed

1/8 teaspoon pepper
2 teaspoons Worcestershire sauce
1 teaspoon grated onion
3 eggs, lightly beaten

Cut bread crosswise into 1-inch slices. Cut crust from slices; use for another purpose. In a medium saucepan, combine butter and cheese. Stir over low heat until both are melted. Stir in dill weed, pepper, Worcestershire sauce and onion. Stirring constantly, add eggs; beat or whisk until well blended. Remove from heat. Dip bread slices into hot mixture, turning to coat both sides. Shake off excess sauce. Place coated slices on 2 large ungreased baking sheets. *Complete now or make ahead.*

To complete now, preheat oven to 350F (175C). Bake coated slices 15 to 18 minutes or until hot and bubbly. To transport, arrange in a single layer in a firm plastic container with a tight-fitting lid. Reheat, if necessary. Serve warm.

To make ahead, freeze coated slices on baking sheets about 2 hours or until solid. When frozen, wrap each slice separately in plastic wrap or foil. Place all wrapped slices in a freezer bag; store in freezer up to 7 days. Transport while still frozen. About 30 minutes before serving time, preheat oven to 350F (175C). Unwrap frozen slices; place on baking sheets in a single layer. Bake frozen slices 20 to 22 minutes or until hot and bubbly. Serve warm. Makes 14 to 16 slices.

Chinese Walnuts

Beware—this tasty snack may be habit-forming.

3 cups water
2 cups walnut halves or pieces
1/4 cup sugar

Vegetable oil for deep-frying
Salt

In a 2-quart saucepan, bring water to boil; add walnuts. Bring to a boil again; boil 1 minute. Immediately pour nuts into a colander. Rinse under hot running water; drain. In a medium bowl, combine warm walnuts and sugar; stir until sugar dissolves. If necessary, cover and let stand about 5 minutes to dissolve sugar. Heat oil in a deep-fryer to 350F (175C) or until a 1-inch bread cube turns golden brown in 65 seconds. With a slotted spoon, add about 1/3 of sugared nuts at a time to hot oil. Fry 2 to 3 minutes or until golden. Place colander over a bowl. Use slotted spoon to remove fried nuts from oil. Place in colander to drain. Sprinkle lightly with salt. Transfer to a platter or paper towels to cool; toss occasionally to separate nuts. *Complete now or make ahead.*

To complete now, place cooled nuts in a decorative serving dish. Serve immediately.

To make ahead, place in a container with a tight-fitting lid. Store at room temperature up to 2 weeks. Makes 2 cups.

— • • • —

Hearty Three-Bean Stew

A stick-to-the-ribs dish to serve with confidence.

1 lb. beef shank
1 lb. ham hock
1 medium onion, chopped
1 carrot, finely chopped
2 medium tomatoes, peeled, seeded, chopped
6 cups water
1 garlic clove, crushed

1/4 teaspoon dried leaf thyme
1 teaspoon salt
1/4 teaspoon pepper
1 (15-oz.) can kidney beans, drained
1 (15-oz.) can garbanzo beans, drained
1 (15-oz.) can lima beans, drained
1/2 lb. smoked sausage, thinly sliced

In a 4- or 6-quart saucepan, combine beef shank, ham hock, onion, carrot, tomatoes, water, garlic, thyme, salt and pepper. Bring to a boil. Cover; gently cook 1-1/2 hours or until meat is very tender. Remove beef shank and ham hock from pan; reserve other ingredients in saucepan. Cut meat from bones; discard bones. Return meat to pan. *Complete now or make ahead.*

To complete now, add beans and sausage. Cover; simmer 15 minutes. Serve hot.

To make ahead, let stew cool. Spoon into a container with a tight-fitting lid. Cover; refrigerate up to 24 hours. Transport stew in covered container. To serve, pour into a saucepan; add beans and sausage. Cover; simmer 15 minutes. Serve hot. Or, let heat in a slow-cooker 3 to 4 hours, adding beans and sausage during last 30 minutes. Makes 8 servings.

Hot Buttered Cider

A warm symbol of hospitality to start off the evening.

6 cups apple cider
1/4 teaspoon ground nutmeg
1/8 teaspoon ground cardamom

2 (3-inch) cinnamon sticks
1/3 cup rum
4 teaspoons butter

In a 2-quart saucepan, combine cider, nutmeg, cardamom and cinnamon. Bring to a boil. Cover; simmer 5 minutes. Set aside to cool. *Complete now or make ahead.*

To complete now, remove cinnamon sticks; heat to boiling point. Remove from heat; stir in rum. Pour into mugs. Top each with about 1/2 teaspoon butter; serve immediately.

To make ahead, pour into a container with a tight-fitting lid; refrigerate up to 4 days. Reheat before serving as directed above. Makes 6 to 8 servings.

● ● ●

Old-Fashioned Orange Sponge Cake

This light citrus-flavored cake travels well.

6 eggs, separated
1 cup granulated sugar
1-3/4 cups all-purpose flour
1/2 teaspoon salt

1/3 cup orange juice
1 teaspoon grated orange peel
1/2 cup granulated sugar
Sifted powdered sugar

Preheat oven to 350F (175C). In a medium bowl, beat egg yolks until thick and lemon colored, about 5 minutes. Gradually beat in 1 cup granulated sugar until smooth. Blend flour and salt; fold into egg-yolk mixture. Fold in orange juice and orange peel. In a large bowl, beat egg whites until foamy. Gradually beat in 1/2 cup granulated sugar, 1 tablespoon at a time. Continue beating until stiff but not dry. Fold egg-yolk mixture into egg-white mixture. Spoon into an ungreased 10-inch tube pan. Bake in preheated oven 35 to 40 minutes or until cake springs back when gently pressed on top. Invert over a wire rack or flat surface; let cool completely in pan. Loosen edges with a spatula; remove from pan. *Complete now or make ahead.*

To complete now, sprinkle cooled cake with powdered sugar. Place in a cake carrier for transporting. Cut into wedges; serve on individual plates.

To make ahead, bake cake up to 2 months ahead; freeze. About 24 hours before serving, thaw at room temperature. Sprinkle with powdered sugar. Serve as directed above. Makes 1 (10-inch) cake.

Video Watching

Country Carousel Loaf
Mustard Mayonnaise
Dilled Onions & Beets
Tin-Roof Ice-Cream Pie

*Y*ou've rented or borrowed a video of one of the old movie classics or a musical video. It's a great way to celebrate an anniversary, birthday or job promotion. Invite 5 or 6 of your friends or co-workers to join the celebration.

Prepare all of your food ahead so you won't have to miss part of the show while you're in the kitchen. Country Carousel Loaf is a spectacular creation, worthy of a very special event. Although it's a main dish, it is round and layered, resembling a beautifully decorated cake. Why not insert the proper number of small candles on top and bring it out in blazing glory for an adult birthday celebration. Everyone can enjoy it while they watch the show. With such a wide variety of meats, seafood, eggs and vegetables in this one dish, the meal is complete when you add a small bowl of Mustard Mayonnaise and a side dish of Dilled Onions & Beets. Tin-Roof Ice-Cream Pie waits in the freezer until you're ready to serve dessert, after the show is over. Serves 6 to 8 people.

MAKE-AHEAD PLAN:

- **Country Carousel Loaf**—Make and freeze Tri-Grain Loaf up to 1 month ahead. Thaw in refrigerator or at room temperature. Assemble loaf no more than 3 hours before serving.
- **Tin-Roof Ice-Cream Pie**—Make and freeze up to 3 days ahead.
- **Mustard Mayonnaise**—Make up to 3 days ahead.
- **Ham-Salad Filling**—Make up to 24 hours ahead.
- **Dilly Deviled Eggs**—Make up to 24 hours ahead.
- **Dilled Onions & Beets**—Make up to 24 hours ahead.

Short-Cuts:

- Purchase a large round loaf of bread from a specialty bakery.
- Substitute hard-cooked eggs for deviled eggs.
- Serve scoops of commercial ice cream instead of making ice-cream pie, or purchase an ice-cream pie.

Dilled Onions & Beets

An intriguing sweet-sour combination.

1 lb. small whole white onions or
   1 (16-oz.) pkg. frozen white onions
1/2 cup red-wine vinegar
2 tablespoons brown sugar
1/4 teaspoon salt

1/8 teaspoon pepper
1/4 teaspoon dried dill weed
1 (16-oz.) can sliced beets, drained
Fresh dill sprigs

Peel fresh onions. In a medium saucepan, cook fresh or frozen onions in water until tender. Drain and cool. In a medium bowl, combine vinegar, brown sugar, salt, pepper and dill weed. Add cooked, drained onions and beets. Toss lightly; cover with plastic wrap or foil. *Complete now or make ahead.*

To complete now, marinate in refrigerator at least 3 hours. Drain; spoon into a serving bowl. Garnish with dill sprigs; serve cold.

To make ahead, marinate in refrigerator up to 24 hours, stirring occasionally. Serve as directed above. Makes 6 to 8 servings.

Dilly Deviled Eggs   *Photo on page 93.*

Eggs are enhanced by exciting dill flavor.

3 or 4 hard-cooked eggs
2 tablespoons mayonnaise
1/2 teaspoon prepared mustard
1 tablespoon vinegar
1/4 teaspoon dried dill weed

1/4 teaspoon salt
1/8 teaspoon pepper
Sliced pimento-stuffed green olives,
   if desired
Chopped fresh dill, if desired

Peel eggs; cut in half lengthwise. Remove hard-cooked egg yolks from whites; set hard-cooked egg whites aside. In a small bowl, mash hard-cooked egg yolks. Stir in mayonnaise, mustard, vinegar, dill weed, salt and pepper. *Complete now or make ahead.*

To complete now, mound egg-yolk mixture into egg-white halves. Or, spoon egg-yolk mixture into a pastry bag; pipe into egg-white halves. Garnish each with an olive slice or chopped dill, if desired. Use to complete Country Carousel Loaf, page 66.

To make ahead, place cooked egg whites in a container large enough to hold them in a single layer; cover airtight. Spoon egg-yolk mixture into a container with a tight-fitting lid. Refrigerate cooked egg whites and egg-yolk mixture up to 24 hours. Assemble as directed above. Makes 6 to 8 deviled-egg halves.

Country Carousel Loaf   *Photo on cover.*

Jumbo meal-in-a-loaf.

1 Tri-Grain Loaf, page 68
Ham-Salad Filling, below
Dilly Deviled Eggs, page 65
Mustard Mayonnaise, opposite
1/4 cup butter or margarine,
    room temperature
Leaf-lettuce leaves
3 oz. Jarlsberg cheese or other Swiss cheese,
    sliced
3 oz. Cheddar cheese or other yellow cheese,
    sliced

1/2 cucumber, thinly sliced
6 to 8 cooked asparagus spears,
    each about 5 inches long
6 to 8 medium shrimp, cooked, shelled,
    deveined
6 or 8 cherry tomatoes
6 or 8 thin smoked-salmon slices (lox)
Fresh dill
Radish roses and onion brushes, if desired

Bake and cool Tri-Grain Loaf. Prepare Ham-Salad Filling, Dilly Deviled Eggs and Mustard Mayonnaise. *Complete now or make ahead.*

To complete now, cut a thin slice off top of loaf to make it level. Then cut bread into 3 equal horizontal slices. Spread bottom slice with butter or margarine, spreading to edge; top with a few lettuce leaves. Spread Ham-Salad Filling over lettuce. Spread both sides of middle bread slice with butter or margarine; place on ham salad. Top with sliced cheeses, letting some of corners extend beyond edge of bread. Butter top of remaining bread slice; place over cheese. Overlap cucumber slices around outer edge of top bread slice. Arrange asparagus spears like spokes of a wheel on top slice. Place a deviled-egg half on edge of loaf between asparagus spears. Place a shrimp around end of each asparagus spear. Arrange lettuce between asparagus spears, forming a ruffle at edges of eggs. Arrange cherry tomatoes on lettuce above eggs and between asparagus spears. Roll up slices of salmon. Arrange salmon rolls like spokes of a wheel between tomatoes and asparagus spears. Garnish center of loaf with fresh dill. Garnish plate with radish roses and onion brushes, if desired. To serve, use wooden skewers to hold layers of bread and top decorations in place. Or, remove some of decorations, placing on individual plates. Cut loaf into wedges. Serve with Mustard Mayonnaise.

To make ahead, wrap cooled Tri-Grain Loaf airtight in freezer wrap; store in freezer up to 1 month. Or, wrap in plastic wrap; let stand at room temperature up to 24 hours. Refrigerate Ham-Salad Filling, Dilly Deviled Eggs and Mustard Mayonnaise up to 24 hours. Assemble loaf as directed above no more than 3 hours before serving. Makes 6 to 8 servings.

●●●

Ham-Salad Filling   *Photo on page 93.*

Equally good when made with leftover baked ham or cooked ham steak.

1/2 lb. lean cooked ham, cubed
1/3 cup mayonnaise

1 teaspoon prepared mustard
2 tablespoons drained sweet-pickle relish

Place ham in a food processor fitted with a metal blade. With quick on/off motions, process until finely chopped. Or, coarsely grind ham in a food grinder. In a small bowl, combine chopped ham, mayonnaise, mustard and pickle relish. *Complete now or make ahead.*

To complete now, use to complete Country Carousel Loaf, above.

To make ahead, spoon filling into a 2-cup container with a tight-fitting lid. Store in refrigerator up to 24 hours. Use as directed above. Makes about 2 cups.

How to Make Country Carousel Loaf

1/Cut off uneven top from loaf. Cut loaf into 3 horizontal slices.

2/Garnish top with cucumber slices and other garnishes as directed.

Mustard Mayonnaise

An extra topping for mayonnaise enthusiasts.

3/4 cup mayonnaise
2 tablespoons Dijon-style mustard
1/8 teaspoon paprika

1/2 teaspoon prepared horseradish
1/8 teaspoon salt

In a small bowl, combine mayonnaise, mustard, paprika, horseradish and salt. Cover with plastic wrap or foil. *Complete now or make ahead.*

To complete now, let stand at room temperature 1 hour to let flavors blend. Serve with Country Carousal Loaf, opposite. Refrigerate any leftovers.

To make ahead, refrigerate 2 to 3 days. Serve as directed above. Makes about 3/4 cup.

Tri-Grain Loaf   *Photo on cover and page 93.*

A hearty three-flour loaf with old-world charm.

2 (1/4-oz.) pkgs. active dry yeast
  (2 tablespoons)
1/2 cup warm water (110F, 45C)
1/4 cup molasses
3/4 cup buttermilk
2 tablespoons butter or margarine,
  room temperature

1 tablespoon caraway seeds
1 teaspoon salt
1-1/4 cups rye flour
1 cup whole-wheat flour
1 to 1-1/2 cups all-purpose flour

In a large bowl, sprinkle yeast over water. Let stand until yeast is softened. Stir in molasses, buttermilk, butter or margarine, caraway seeds, salt and rye flour. Beat until smooth. Stir in whole-wheat flour and enough all-purpose flour to make a medium-stiff dough. On a lightly floured surface, knead 8 to 10 minutes or until smooth. Clean and grease bowl. Place kneaded dough in bowl, turning to grease all sides. Cover; let rise in a warm place, free from drafts, 1 hour or until doubled in bulk. Grease a large baking sheet. Punch down dough; shape into a ball. Flatten ball, making a round 7-inch loaf about 1-1/4 inches thick. Place on greased baking sheet. Make several parallel slashes, about 1/2 inch deep, in top of loaf. Cover; let rise 40 to 50 minutes or until doubled in bulk. Preheat oven to 350F (175C). Bake in preheated oven 35 minutes. Remove from baking sheet; cool on a wire rack. *Complete now or make ahead.*

To complete now, use immediately to make Country Carousel Loaf, page 66.

To make ahead, bake loaf up to 1 month ahead. Wrap airtight in freezer wrap. Store in freezer; thaw in refrigerator 24 hours before assembling, or thaw at room temperature. Use to make Country Carousel Loaf. Makes 1 (9-inch) round loaf.

Tin-Roof Ice-Cream Pie

Guaranteed to be the top dessert of the year by all lovers of chocolate and peanuts.

24 cream-filled chocolate-sandwich cookies
2 tablespoons butter or margarine, melted
1/3 cup chopped peanuts
1 qt. vanilla ice cream, slightly softened

1/2 cup chocolate-fudge ice-cream topping
Whipped cream
Whole or halved peanuts

In a blender or food processor fitted with a metal blade, process cookies until crumbs form. In a medium bowl, combine cookie crumbs, butter or margarine and chopped peanuts. Press into bottom and up side of 9-inch pie pan. Refrigerate at least 1 hour. Press 1/2 of ice cream over chilled crust. Spoon 1/2 of fudge topping over ice cream. Top with remaining ice cream; then remaining topping. *Complete now or make ahead.*

To complete now, cover with foil or plastic wrap; freeze at least 4 hours or until firm. Decorate with swirls or rosettes of whipped cream. Sprinkle whole or halved peanuts over whipped cream. To serve, let frozen cake stand in refrigerator 10 minutes before cutting. Cut into 6 to 8 wedges; place wedges on individual plates.

To make ahead, cover with foil; freeze up to 3 days. Decorate at serving time or up to 24 hours ahead. Refrigerate until served; let stand 10 minutes before cutting. Makes 6 to 8 servings.

Delta Feast

Shrimp Rémoulade
Seafood & Sausage Gumbo
Bayou Jambalaya
Delta Bean Pot
French Bread   Butter
Praline Parfaits

Thoughts of a Delta Feast bring fond memories of fabulous foods from New Orleans. We have recreated our versions of those nostalgic foods that have become a part of our national heritage. Then we added a few modern touches. The result is a mouthwatering combination of flavors borrowed from Cajun and Creole culinary traditions.

The menu naturally lends itself to a traditional sit-down dinner, starting with an appetizer of Shrimp Rémoulade. Although Bayou Jambalaya is actually hearty enough to be a one-dish meal, be sure to include Seafood & Sausage Gumbo as a soup course between the appetizer and main dish. If possible, obtain traditional smoked sausage called *andouille*. If it is not available, use any good smoked pork sausage. The dishes are moderately spiced so everyone should be able to enjoy this delicious food. Serves 6 people.

MAKE-AHEAD PLAN:

- **Praline Parfaits**—Freeze up to 4 days ahead.
- **Shrimp Rémoulade**—Make sauce up to 24 hours ahead. Combine sauce and shrimp just before serving.
- **Seafood & Sausage Gumbo**—Make up to 24 hours ahead; reheat before serving.
- **Bayou Jambalaya**—Make up to 24 hours ahead; reheat before serving.
- **Delta Bean Pot**—Make up to 24 hours ahead or early the day of your party; keep hot in an electric slow-cooker.

Short-Cuts:

- Serve scoops of commercial praline-flavored ice cream instead of making parfaits.
- Omit Delta Bean Pot.

Bayou Jambalaya

Adjust the heat level of this popular dish by regulating the amount of red pepper used.

2 tablespoons butter or margarine
2 tablespoons vegetable oil
1 (3- to 3-1/2-lb.) broiler-fryer, cut up
1 cup uncooked long-grain white rice
1 onion, chopped
1 medium, green bell pepper, chopped
2 celery stalks, chopped
1 garlic clove, crushed

1/2 lb. smoked sausage links,
    sliced about 1/4 inch thick
2 cups beef broth or bouillon
1/2 teaspoon chili powder or to taste
1 teaspoon salt
1/8 teaspoon red (cayenne) pepper or to taste
1/4 teaspoon dried leaf thyme

In a large skillet or Dutch oven, melt butter or margarine; add oil. Add chicken; brown on both sides. Remove chicken from pan. Stir rice into drippings in pan; stirring constantly, cook until rice is a light golden color. Add onion, bell pepper, celery, garlic and sausage. Stir in broth or bouillon, chili powder, salt, red pepper and thyme. Return browned chicken to pan. Cover; cook 40 minutes over low heat, stirring occasionally. *Complete now or make ahead.*

To complete now, serve in a colorful skillet, or spoon into a large platter or serving dish; serve hot.

To make ahead, place chicken and sauce in a nonmetal container with a tight-fitting lid. Refrigerate up to 24 hours. Reheat 15 to 20 minutes or until hot. Serve as directed above. Makes 6 servings.

Delta Bean Pot

This popular hearty dish is traditionally served with rice.

1 lb. dried lima beans or red beans
6 cups water
1 onion, chopped
1/2 cup chopped celery
1/2 cup chopped green bell pepper
1 garlic clove, crushed

1-1/2 to 2 lbs. ham hocks
1 teaspoon salt
1/8 teaspoon dried red peppers, crushed
1/2 teaspoon dried leaf oregano
2 to 3 cups hot cooked long-grain white rice,
    if desired

In a large heavy saucepan, bring beans and water to a boil; boil 2 minutes. Remove from heat; let stand 1 hour. Add onion, celery, bell pepper, garlic and ham hocks. Cover and simmer over low heat 1 hour. Remove ham hocks; discard skin, fat and bones. Chop meat into 1/2-inch pieces; return chopped ham to saucepan. Stir in salt, red pepper and oregano; cover tightly. Continue simmering over low heat 1 hour longer or until beans are tender, stirring several times. For a less soupy texture, remove lid; cook 15 to 20 minutes longer, stirring occasionally. *Complete now or make ahead.*

To complete now, spoon a little cooked rice into each individual soup bowl, if desired. Ladle soup over rice.

To make ahead, keep hot in a covered slow-cooker on low heat 3 to 4 hours. Or, refrigerate cooked beans overnight. Reheat in a large heavy saucepan over low heat. Serve as directed above. Makes 6 servings.

How to Make Seafood & Sausage Gumbo

1/Stirring constantly with a wooden spoon, cook until mixture is color of milk chocolate.

2/Spoon about 1/2 cup rice in center of each soup bowl. Ladle gumbo over rice.

Seafood & Sausage Gumbo

Browning the flour and oil to form a flavorful roux is the secret to the marvelous flavor.

1/2 cup vegetable oil
1/2 cup all-purpose flour
1 large onion, chopped
1 cup chopped celery
1 green bell pepper, chopped
1/2 teaspoon paprika
1/2 teaspoon salt
1/4 teaspoon black pepper
1/8 teaspoon red (cayenne) pepper

1/2 teaspoon dried leaf thyme
1 garlic clove, crushed
1 tomato, peeled, seeded, chopped
1/4 lb. smoked pork sausage, chopped
5 cups chicken broth or bouillon
1/2 lb. uncooked small or medium shrimp, shelled, deveined
1/4 lb. shredded crabmeat
3 cups hot cooked long-grain white rice

In a heavy 4-quart saucepan, heat oil; gradually add flour. Stirring constantly with a wooden spoon, cook over medium heat until mixture is the color of milk chocolate, 5 to 10 minutes. Remove from heat; add onion, celery, bell pepper, paprika, salt, black pepper, red pepper, thyme and garlic. Reduce heat; stirring occasionally, cook 5 minutes or until vegetables are softened. Stir in tomato, smoked sausage and broth or bouillon. Stirring occasionally, simmer uncovered at medium heat 40 minutes. *Complete now or make ahead.*

To complete now, add shrimp and crabmeat. Cook 5 minutes or until shrimp turn pink. Spoon about 1/2 cup rice in center of each of 6 large soup bowls. Ladle gumbo over rice. Serve hot.

To make ahead, pour tomato mixture into a large bowl. Cover and refrigerate up to 24 hours. To reheat, bring to a simmer. Add shrimp and crabmeat. Cook 5 minutes or until shrimp turn pink. Serve as directed above. Makes 6 servings.

Shrimp Rémoulade

A memorable appetizer based on a favorite classic recipe from New Orleans.

2 tablespoons lemon juice
2 tablespoons tarragon vinegar
1/2 teaspoon salt
1/4 teaspoon pepper
1/4 teaspoon paprika
1 tablespoon prepared spicy brown mustard
1 teaspoon Worcestershire sauce
1 tablespoon prepared horseradish
1 tablespoon ketchup

Dash hot-pepper sauce
1/2 cup vegetable oil
1 lb. small or medium shrimp, cooked,
    shelled, deveined
1/4 cup chopped celery
1 shallot, finely chopped
Lettuce
2 hard-cooked eggs, sliced
10 or 12 pitted ripe olives

In a blender or food processor fitted with a metal blade, combine lemon juice, vinegar, salt, pepper, paprika, mustard, Worcestershire sauce, horseradish, ketchup and hot-pepper sauce. Gradually add oil while processing. Continue processing until smooth and thick. In a small bowl, combine shrimp, celery and shallot. *Complete now or make ahead.*

To complete now, mix dressing and shrimp mixture. Line individual sherbet glasses or salad plates with lettuce. Spoon equal amounts of shrimp mixture into each lettuce-lined glass or plate. Garnish with hard-cooked-egg slices and olives.

To make ahead, place dressing and shrimp mixture in separate containers with tight-fitting lids. Refrigerate up to 24 hours. Combine as directed above. Makes 6 servings.

Praline Parfaits

An elegant dessert with minimum effort.

3/4 cup lightly packed brown sugar
1/2 cup light corn syrup
1/2 cup half and half
2 tablespoons butter or margarine

1/2 teaspoon vanilla extract
1 qt. vanilla-flavored ice cream
1/2 cup coarsely chopped pecans
Whipped cream

In a small saucepan, combine brown sugar, corn syrup and half and half. Stirring constantly, simmer about 5 minutes or until thickened. Remove from heat; stir in butter or margarine and vanilla. Refrigerate until cool. Spoon alternate layers of cooled sauce, ice cream and pecans into parfait or wine glasses. *Complete now or make ahead.*

To complete now, freeze at least 4 hours. Top each serving with a swirl of whipped cream.

To make ahead, freeze 3 to 4 days. Serve as directed above. Makes 6 to 8 servings.

Dim Sum Celebration

Shrimp Dumplings
Pork Potstickers
Oriental-Style Mustard Sauce
Oriental-Style Barbecued Ribs
Make-Ahead Rice
Chicken-Filled Steamed Buns
Tea-Time Custard Tarts
Hot Tea   Chinese Beer

The Chinese have been enjoying dim sum in tea houses for centuries. Traditionally, dim sum consists of small morsels that are similar to appetizers. In restaurants, waitresses bring carts of these tidbits to each table and you pick out the ones you prefer. We have selected a variety for you to try. These are small and time-consuming to make so we've suggested that you freeze some and refrigerate others. We've given you more recipes than you need. Choose your favorites, omitting one or two dishes, and at least 12 people will have good reason to celebrate. It's fun to serve Chinese beer in addition to traditional hot tea. Serves 12 people.

MAKE-AHEAD PLAN:

- **Pork Potstickers**—Fill and freeze up to 1 month ahead. Cook frozen potstickers immediately before serving.
- **Shrimp Dumplings**—Fill and freeze dumplings up to 1 month. Steam frozen dumplings immediately before serving.
- **Chicken-Filled Chinese Steamed Buns**—Make and freeze up to 1 month ahead. Steam immediately before serving.
- **Oriental-Style Mustard Sauce**—Prepare up to 7 days ahead.
- **Oriental-Style Barbecued Riblets**—Marinate ribs at least 4 hours; bake 1-1/2 hours. Refrigerate ribs and marinade up to 24 hours. Bake 50 to 60 minutes before serving.
- **Make-Ahead Rice**—Cook up to 24 hours ahead; reheat about 10 minutes before serving.
- **Tea-Time Custard Tarts**—Bake up to 24 hours ahead. Refrigerate until served.

Short-Cuts:

- Purchase 2 or 3 similar appetizers from local Chinese restaurants. Omit several of our recipes.
- Purchase similar mustard sauce at a deli.
- Purchase custard tarts or Chinese almond cookies.
- Use instant rice instead of Make-Ahead Rice.

Shrimp Dumplings

Photo on pages 102-103.

Combination of shrimp and water chestnuts creates a popular appetizer.

1/2 lb. shrimp, cooked, shelled, deveined, finely chopped
6 water chestnuts, minced
6 mushrooms, finely chopped
1 green onion, finely chopped
1 egg, lightly beaten

1 tablespoon soy sauce
1 tablespoon honey
1/4 teaspoon salt
2 teaspoons sesame oil
36 (3-inch) round or square won-ton skins

In a medium bowl, combine shrimp, water chestnuts, mushrooms and green onion. Stir in egg, soy sauce, honey, salt and sesame oil. Keep won-ton skins covered to prevent drying. Cut square won-ton skins into 3-inch-diameter circles. Working with 1 won-ton skin at a time, spoon 2 teaspoons mixture onto center. Bring edge up around filling on all sides, pleating edge. Press pleats together, leaving top open. Lightly cover filled dumplings to prevent drying. *Complete now or make ahead.*

To complete now, pour water about 1 inch deep in a wok or 12-inch skillet; bring to a boil. Arrange dumplings on a steamer rack, open-side up, not touching. Place filled rack in wok or skillet; cover and steam over low heat 10 to 15 minutes or until filling is warmed and won tons are translucent. Arrange on a platter or serving dish; serve warm.

To make ahead, arrange filled dumplings, open-side up, in a single layer on an ungreased baking sheet. Freeze until firm. Place frozen dumplings in a freezer bag or firm freezer container with a tight-fitting lid; seal bag or container. Freeze up to 1 month. About 30 minutes before serving, bring 1 inch water to a boil in a wok or 12-inch skillet. Arrange frozen dumplings on a steamer rack, open-side up, not touching. Place filled rack in wok or skillet; cover and steam over low heat 15 to 20 minutes or until filling is warmed and won tons are translucent. Serve as directed above. Makes about 36 dumplings.

Oriental-Style Mustard Sauce

Photo on pages 102-103.

Just the right accent for dim sum.

3 tablespoons dry mustard
1/8 teaspoon ground ginger
2 tablespoons hot water

1/4 cup soy sauce
1/2 cup dairy sour cream

In a small bowl, combine dry mustard and ginger. Stir in hot water, a little at a time; stir until smooth. Stir in soy sauce. Spoon sour cream into another small bowl. Gradually stir mustard mixture into sour cream; stir until blended. *Complete now or make ahead.*

To complete now, refrigerate at least 1 hour to let flavors blend. To serve, spoon into a small serving dish. Serve with dim sum.

To make ahead, spoon mustard into a small container with a tight-fitting lid; refrigerate up to 7 days. Serve as directed above. Makes 2/3 cup.

Dim Sum Celebration

A sample of popular Chinese appetizers that you can reproduce in your own kitchen. Copy the traditional Chinese tea houses by including a combination of contrasting textures, colors and flavors.

Design an out-of-the-ordinary meal with an assortment of these tasty morsels.

Clockwise from top: Oriental-Style Barbecued Ribs, page 105, Make-Ahead Rice, page 105, Shrimp Dumplings, page 101, Chicken-Filled Steamed Buns, page 104, Oriental Mustard Sauce, page 101, and Pork Potstickers, page 106.

Chicken-Filled Steamed Buns

Photo on pages 102-103.

Flavors similar to those found in famous Chinese restaurants.

6 chicken-breast halves, skinned, boned
2 tablespoons soy sauce
2 tablespoons dry white wine
2 tablespoons hoisin sauce
2 tablespoons ketchup
2 tablespoons honey
1 garlic clove, minced

1 tablespoon minced gingerroot
1/4 teaspoon ground allspice or
   five-spice powder
2 tablespoons vegetable oil
1/2 cup chicken broth or bouillon
1 tablespoon cornstarch
2 tablespoons water

Dough:
1 (1/4-oz.) pkg. active dry yeast
   (1 tablespoon)
1 cup warm water (110F, 45C)

3 cups all-purpose flour
2 tablespoons sugar
1 tablespoon vegetable oil

Finely chop chicken breasts; place in a 9" x 5" glass loaf pan. In a small bowl, combine soy sauce, wine, hoisin sauce, ketchup, honey, garlic, gingerroot and allspice or five-spice powder. Pour over chicken; stir to distribute. Cover with foil or plastic wrap; refrigerate at least 4 hours or overnight. In a heavy, medium skillet, heat oil; add chicken and marinade. Stirring constantly, cook over medium heat 2 to 3 minutes or until chicken is tender. Add broth or bouillon. In a small bowl, dissolve cornstarch in 2 tablespoons water. Stir into chicken mixture; stirring constantly, cook over medium-high heat 3 to 4 minutes or until translucent. Cool slightly; refrigerate. Prepare Dough. Cut 16 (4-inch) squares of waxed paper; set aside. Punch down dough; let stand 5 minutes. With a sharp knife, cut dough in half; then cut each half in 8 pieces. Shape each piece into a ball; roll each ball into a 4-inch circle with edges thinner than center. To fill buns, hold a dough circle in the palm of 1 hand in a cupping shape. Spoon about 1-1/2 tablespoons filling in center. Gather edge of dough up over top of filling. Slightly twist gathered edge; gently pinch to seal. If necessary, dampen edge with water. Repeat with remaining dough and filling. Place each shaped bun, sealed-side down, on a waxed-paper square. Place buns, waxed-paper-side down, on a large ungreased baking sheet. *Complete now or make ahead.*

To make Dough, in a 2-cup measure, sprinkle yeast over warm water; stir to dissolve. In a large bowl, combine flour and sugar. Make a well in center; pour in dissolved yeast and oil. Stir until blended. Turn out onto a lightly floured surface; knead about 5 minutes or until smooth and elastic. Clean and grease bowl; place dough in bowl, turning to grease all sides. Cover with a clean cloth; let rise in a warm place, free from drafts, about 1 hour or until doubled in bulk.

To complete now, cover filled buns with a dry cloth; let rise until doubled in bulk, about 45 minutes. Pour water 1 inch deep in a wok or 12-inch skillet; bring to a boil. Arrange buns, at least 1 inch apart, on a steamer rack; do not crowd. Place filled steamer rack over boiling water. Cover with foil; steam over low heat 20 minutes. Remove waxed paper from cooked buns; serve hot.

To make ahead, place baking sheet in freezer; freeze buns until firm. Keeping frozen buns on waxed-paper squares, place in freezer bags; seal bags. Freeze up to 1 month. About 2 hours before serving, arrange frozen buns, waxed-paper-side down, on a baking sheet. Cover with a dry cloth; let rise in a warm place, free from drafts, until dough is doubled in bulk, about 1-1/2 hours. Steam and serve as directed above. Makes 16 steamed buns.

Oriental-Style Barbecued Ribs

Photo on pages 102-103.

A magical combination of seasonings to enhance ribs.

Oriental-Style Mustard Sauce, page 101
1/2 recipe Make-Ahead Rice, below
3 to 4 lbs. pork-loin back ribs,
   halved crosswise
1/3 cup hoisin sauce
3 tablespoons honey
3 tablespoons soy sauce
1 tablespoon sesame oil

3 green onions, minced
1 tablespoon minced gingerroot
1 garlic clove, crushed
3 tablespoons wine vinegar
Sesame seeds
Lettuce leaves
Young, tender Chinese pea pods

Prepare Oriental-Style Mustard Sauce and Make-Ahead Rice; set aside. Cut ribs into 1-rib servings; arrange in a single layer in a 13" x 9" baking dish. In a medium bowl, combine hoisin sauce, honey, soy sauce, sesame oil, green onions, gingerroot, garlic and vinegar. Pour over ribs. Cover with foil or plastic wrap; refrigerate at least 4 hours or overnight. Drain; reserve marinade. Arrange marinated ribs in a single layer on broiler rack on a broiler pan. Place broiler pan in cold oven. Pour boiling water in broiler pan until 3/4 full or nearly to top; cover with foil. Turn oven to 300F (150C). Bake 1-1/2 hours. *Complete now or make ahead.*

To complete now, remove foil. Increase heat to 350F (175C). Brush partially baked ribs with marinade. Bake 35 to 45 minutes or until golden brown. Turn and brush with marinade at least once during final baking. Sprinkle tops of baked ribs with sesame seeds. To serve, line a platter or serving dish with lettuce leaves. Arrange sesame-seed-topped ribs like spokes of a wheel around outer edge of platter or dish. Arrange Chinese pea pods like spokes of a wheel on center, slightly overlapping ribs and lettuce. Spoon Make-Ahead Rice onto pea pods. Serve hot with Oriental-Style Mustard Sauce.

To make ahead, cool baked ribs. Place cooled ribs in a rigid plastic container with a tight-fitting lid. Pour reserved marinade into a container with a tight-fitting lid. Refrigerate ribs and reserved marinade up to 24 hours. About 1 hour before serving, place refrigerated baked ribs in a 13" x 9" baking dish; brush with reserved marinade. Bake 50 to 60 minutes in a 350F (175C) oven, turning and brushing with marinade at least once. Sprinkle tops of baked ribs with sesame seeds. Serve as directed above. Makes 12 appetizer servings.

Make-Ahead Rice

Photo on pages 102-103.

When serving time rolls around, the rice is a cinch.

1 qt. water (4 cups)
2 cups uncooked long-grain white rice

1 teaspoon salt
2 tablespoons vegetable oil

Bring water to boil in a heavy 3-quart saucepan with a tight-fitting lid. Stir in rice and salt. Bring back to a boil; cover. Reduce heat; simmer 20 minutes or until rice is tender and water is absorbed. Remove from heat. *Complete now or make ahead.*

To complete now, spoon rice into a serving bowl. Serve alone or with other dishes.

To make ahead, add oil; toss to distribute and coat rice. Spoon into a large bowl; cover with foil or plastic wrap; refrigerate up to 24 hours. About 15 minutes before serving, pour water 1 inch deep in a 3-quart saucepan; bring to a boil. Place cooked rice in a metal strainer; place over boiling water. Cover, placing lid slightly ajar; let water simmer over low heat 7 to 10 minutes or until rice is hot. Serve as directed above. Makes 12 (1/2-cup) servings.

Pork Potstickers

Photo on pages 102-103.

Tasty traditional dim sum morsels.

1 tablespoon cornstarch	1 tablespoon brown sugar
2 tablespoons dry white wine	1/4 teaspoon salt
1 tablespoon vegetable oil	1/8 teaspoon pepper
1/2 lb. lean uncooked pork, finely chopped	36 (3-inch) round or square won-ton skins
2 green onions, minced	2 tablespoons vegetable oil
1 cup minced cabbage	1/2 cup chicken broth or bouillon
1 tablespoon soy sauce	Oriental-Style Mustard Sauce, page 103

In a small bowl, dissolve cornstarch in wine; set aside. In a medium skillet, heat 1 tablespoon oil. Add pork; cook and stir 3 or 4 minutes or until no longer pink. Stir in green onions, cabbage, soy sauce, brown sugar, salt and pepper. Stir cornstarch mixture; stir into pork mixture. Stirring constantly, cook over medium heat until translucent. Let cool slightly. Cut square won-ton skins into 3-inch-diameter rounds. Keep won-ton skins covered to prevent drying. Working with 1 won-ton skin at a time, spoon 2 teaspoons of the pork mixture off center. Moisten edges of skin with water. Bring opposite side of skin up over filling forming a semicircle. Pinch edges to seal; then make 3 or 4 tucks along sealed edge. Holding a potsticker on tucked edge, place potsticker, tucked-edge up, on a flat surface. Still holding tucked edge, press down on filled part of potsticker with your fingers until it sits flat. Repeat until remaining skins are filled and flattened. *Complete now or make ahead.*

To complete now, pour 2 tablespoons oil into a 12-inch skillet. Place 6 potstickers in skillet, tucked-edge up, not touching. Cook uncovered until bottoms are golden brown; remove from skillet. Repeat with remaining potstickers, cooking 6 at a time. Return browned potstickers to skillet. Pour broth or bouillon into skillet. Cover; cook over low heat 10 minutes or until potstickers are translucent. Remove from skillet; arrange on a platter or serving dish. Serve warm with Oriental-Style Mustard Sauce.

To make ahead, place potstickers on a baking sheet; cover with foil or plastic wrap. Refrigerate overnight or freeze until firm. Place frozen potstickers in a freezer bag; seal. Freeze up to 1 month. About 30 minutes before serving, heat 2 tablespoons oil in a 12-inch skillet. Arrange 6 refrigerated or frozen potstickers in skillet, seam-side up, not touching. Cook uncovered until bottoms are golden brown; remove from skillet. Repeat with remaining potstickers, cooking 6 at a time. Return browned potstickers to skillet. Pour broth or bouillon into skillet. Cover; cook over low heat 15 minutes or until potstickers are translucent. Serve as directed above. Makes about 36 potstickers.

How to Make Pork Potstickers

1/Spoon pork mixture off center on won-ton skins. Brush edges with water.

2/Pinch edges to seal. Make 3 or 4 tucks along sealed edge.

Tea-Time Custard Tarts

An appropriate grand finale to a dim sum luncheon.

2 cups all-purpose flour
1 teaspoon salt
2/3 cup vegetable shortening
6 to 7 tablespoons water
1 egg white, lightly beaten
1 egg yolk, lightly beaten

3 whole eggs, lightly beaten
2/3 cup sugar
1 (5.33-oz.) can evaporated milk
1/2 cup whole milk
1/2 teaspoon vanilla extract
1/8 teaspoon almond extract

In a medium bowl, combine flour and salt. Using a pastry blender or 2 knives, cut in shortening until mixture resembles coarse crumbs. Gradually stir in water until mixture forms a ball. On a lightly floured surface, roll out dough until 1/8 inch thick. Cut into 17 or 18 (4-1/2-inch-diameter) circles. Preheat oven to 425F (220C). Ease pastry circles into 2-3/4″ x 1-1/4″ tart pans. Trim edges even with pan rims; brush with egg white. Place tart pans on a baking sheet. Bake in preheated oven 7 minutes. Remove from oven. Reduce oven temperature to 350F (175C). In a large bowl, combine egg yolk, whole eggs and sugar. Stir in evaporated milk, whole milk, vanilla and almond extract. Spoon into baked crusts. Bake 15 to 20 minutes or until a knife inserted in center comes out clean. Cool to room temperature. *Complete now or make ahead.*

To complete now, arrange cooled tarts on a platter or serving plate.

To make ahead, refrigerate cooled tarts up to 24 hours. Serve as directed above. Makes 17 or 18 tarts.

Fiesta Bon Voyage

Mexican Beer   Margaritas
Tri-Color Pepper Wedges
Nachos Grande
Fresh-Corn & Chicken Tamales
Tacos   Refried Beans
Fresh Salsa
Flour or Corn Tortillas   Butter
Carmen's Tropical-Flan Ring

Whether your friends are leaving for a South-of-the-Border vacation or to other exciting parts of the world, send them off in a festive mood with a Fiesta Bon Voyage. Begin the celebration in the living room with Tri-Color Pepper Wedges and Nachos Grande accompanied by glasses of Mexican Beer or Margaritas. Have lots of cocktail napkins handy when everybody dips into the pizza-size nachos.

Then move to the dining room for a buffet-style Mexican feast. Easy make-ahead tacos require no recipe. Have bowls of taco-flavored fried hamburger, chopped onions, chopped tomatoes and shredded yellow or white cheese ready to be spooned into ready-to-eat taco shells. Each person is on his or her own, putting tacos together and enjoying homemade Fresh-Corn & Chicken Tamales.

The hearty and filling menu is designed to satisfy most Mexican-food enthusiasts. Serves 10 to 12 people.

MAKE-AHEAD PLAN:

- **Fresh Salsa**—Make up to 24 hours ahead.
- **Fresh-Corn & Chicken Tamales**—Prepare up to 24 hours ahead. Steam before serving.
- **Tri-Color Pepper Wedges**—Make up to 24 hours ahead.
- **Beer or Margaritas**—Refrigerate beer and ingredients for Margaritas up to 24 hours. Finish Margaritas as guests arrive.
- **Carmen's Tropical-Flan Ring**—Make custard ring up to 24 hours ahead, but at least 8 hours before serving. Peel and slice fruits 3 to 4 hours before serving; refrigerate separately.
- **Nachos Grande**—Refrigerate 6 to 8 hours. Broil immediately before serving.

Short-Cuts:

- Use canned refried beans; add cheese before heating.
- Use canned salsa.
- Use purchased taco shells
- Buy preshredded Cheddar cheese and Monterey Jack cheese.

Tri-Color Pepper Wedges   *Photo on pages 110-111.*

Three different peppers make a dramatic display, but any combination is tasty.

1 (8-oz.) pkg. cream cheese,
    room temperature
8 oz. ricotta cheese (1 cup)
2 teaspoons prepared horseradish
1 teaspoon prepared mustard
1/4 teaspoon black pepper
1/2 teaspoon seasoned salt
1 (2-1/2-oz.) pkg. thinly sliced smoked or
    dried beef, finely chopped

2 radishes, minced
1 tablespoon minced green onion
1 medium, green bell pepper
1 medium, red bell pepper
1 medium, yellow bell pepper
Halved ripe-olive slices
Pimento strips

In a medium bowl, blender or food processor fitted with a metal blade, beat or process cream cheese, ricotta cheese, horseradish, mustard, black pepper and seasoned salt until smooth. Stir in beef, radishes and green onion; set aside. Remove stems of peppers by cutting a 1-inch circle around tops. Remove seeds from stem; reserve stems. Use a spoon to scoop out seeds and membrane from inside peppers. Spoon cheese mixture into peppers; top with reserved stems. Wrap each filled pepper in plastic wrap or place each in a small plastic bag; seal. *Complete now or make ahead.*

To complete now, refrigerate at least 2 hours. To serve, remove and discard pepper stems. Cut each stuffed pepper in half lengthwise; cut each half-pepper into 4 wedges. Arrange on a tray; garnish with olive slices and pimento strips.

To make ahead, refrigerate up to 24 hours. Cut and serve as directed above. Makes 24 wedges.

Nachos Grande

Choose your own heat-level by using mild green chilies or more spicy jalapeños.

4 cups fried corn-tortilla pieces or chips
    (about 4 oz.)
2 cups shredded Monterey Jack cheese (8 oz.)
1 cup shredded sharp Cheddar cheese (4 oz.)
1 (4-oz.) can green chilies or jalapeños,
    chopped, drained
1/4 cup chopped green onions

1/2 cup dairy sour cream
1/4 cup sliced pitted ripe olives
1 large ripe avocado, chopped, tossed with
    1 tablespoon lemon juice
1 tomato, chopped
Chopped cilantro
Taco sauce, if desired

Arrange tortilla pieces or chips on a 12-inch pizza pan. Sprinkle with Monterey Jack cheese and Cheddar cheese. Top with chilies and green onion. *Complete now or make ahead.*

To complete now, preheat broiler. Place pan 5 to 6 inches from heat; broil 2 to 3 minutes or until cheese melts. Immediately top with sour cream, olives, avocado and tomato. Sprinkle with cilantro. Serve hot with taco sauce, if desired.

To make ahead, cover tightly with foil or plastic wrap; refrigerate 6 to 8 hours. Broil, garnish and serve as directed above. Makes 10 to 12 appetizer servings.

Fiesta Bon Voyage

A show-stopper beginning to your Bon Voyage Party! Arrange alternating stuffed red, green and yellow bell-pepper wedges on a large tray. All have the same filling, so let guests pick up their favorite color while waiting for the main dish.

Tri-Color Pepper Wedges, page 109

Fresh-Corn & Chicken Tamales

Fresh-corn flavor makes the great difference.

9 ears corn in husks
3/4 cup yellow cornmeal
3 tablespoons vegetable shortening
2 tablespoons sugar
2 teaspoons salt

3 cups diced cooked chicken
1-1/2 cups diced Cheddar cheese (6 oz.)
1/3 cup minced canned green chilies
1 tablespoon minced onion

Remove husks and silk from corn, reserving 40 to 60 of largest husks. Cut corn kernels off cobs; discard cobs. In a blender or food processor fitted with a metal blade, process 2 cups corn kernels at a time until finely chopped. In a large bowl, combine chopped corn, cornmeal, shortening, sugar and salt. Stir until blended. In a medium bowl, combine chicken, cheese, chilies and onion. Place 2 or 3 corn husks on a flat surface with long edges overlapping. Spread 3 tablespoons corn mixture in center of husks making a 5" x 4" rectangle. Top with 1/3 cup chicken mixture. Spread another 3 tablespoons corn mixture over chicken mixture. Fold sides of husks over filling, overlapping to completely encase filling. Tie both open ends of husks securely with string. Repeat until remaining tamales are assembled. *Complete now or make ahead.*

To complete now, pour water 1 inch deep in a Dutch oven or kettle; bring water to a boil. Place rack over boiling water; lay tamales flat on rack, overlapping if necessary. Cover and steam 60 to 70 minutes or until tamales are firm when touched. Remove from pot; serve hot in husks.

To make ahead, place uncooked tamales in a container with a tight-fitting lid; refrigerate up to 24 hours. Cook tamales about 1-1/2 hours; serve as directed above. Makes 12 tamales.

Variations

If corn is already husked, purchase dried husks. Soak dried husks in hot water 1 hour to soften.

Tamales in Foil: Cut 12 (9" x 7") pieces of foil. Spread with corn mixture and chicken mixture as directed above. Fold foil crosswise over filling. Fold all edges twice to make a secure package. Stand tamales, folded-edge down, on a rack over boiling water. Cover pot; steam 1 hour or until dough pulls away from foil easily.

• ● •

Fresh Salsa

A lively relish to enhance tacos and tamales.

2 fresh California green chilies
1 large tomato, chopped
1 onion, chopped
1/4 cup loosely packed chopped cilantro

1/2 teaspoon salt
2 tablespoons white vinegar
1/2 teaspoon celery seeds

To handle fresh chilies, cover your hands with rubber or plastic gloves. After handling, do not touch your face or eyes. Cut chilies in thin strips; discard seeds. Finely chop chilies. In a medium bowl, combine chopped chilies, tomato, onion, cilantro, salt, vinegar and celery seeds. Cover with foil or plastic wrap. *Complete now or make ahead.*

To complete now, refrigerate at least 2 hours to let flavors blend; serve cold.

To make ahead, refrigerate up to 24 hours; serve cold. Makes 1-1/2 cups.

How to Make Fresh-Corn & Chicken Tamales

1/Spread corn mixture over center of husks. Top with some of chicken mixture and more of corn mixture.

2/Fold side husks over filling, overlapping to completely encase filling. Tie ends with string.

Carmen's Tropical Flan Ring

A custard-like cream dessert surrounded by tropical fruits.

3/4 cup sugar
6 eggs, lightly beaten
1-1/2 pints milk or half and half (3 cups)
1/3 cup sugar
1/2 cup flaked coconut

1 teaspoon vanilla extract
2 papayas, peeled, sliced
1 pineapple, peeled, cubed
2 kiwifruit, peeled, sliced

In a heavy medium skillet, heat 3/4 cup sugar, stirring constantly, until sugar melts and turns golden. Immediately pour into bottom of a 1-1/2-inch-deep round 9-inch cake pan; set aside. Preheat oven to 325F (165C). In a medium bowl, combine eggs, milk or half and half, 1/3 cup sugar, coconut and vanilla. Pour over caramelized sugar in mold. Place filled mold in a 13" x 10" broiler pan. Pour boiling water about 1 inch deep in broiler pan around mold. Bake in preheated oven 40 to 45 minutes or until a knife inserted off center comes out clean. Remove mold from water; let stand 15 minutes. Cover with foil or plastic wrap. *Complete now or make ahead.*

To complete now, refrigerate at least 8 hours. To serve, loosen edge with a spatula. Invert mold onto a large platter or tray with a rim; remove pan. Place platter with flan on a larger tray. Arrange fruits on outer tray around baked flan; serve cold.

To make ahead, refrigerate up to 24 hours. Serve as directed above. Makes 10 to 12 servings.

Dreaming of the Tropics

Caribbean Connection
Sesame Chicken Wings
Aloha Ham Bites
Mariner's Filo Roll-Ups
Oasis Coleslaw
South-Seas Loaf   Butter
Trade-Winds Cake

Get out the travel folders, posters and pictures of swaying palm trees, white sandy beaches and coves where crystal-clear blue water washes the shore. If your backyard is void of tropical leaves, order a few ti leaves and blossoms from the florist. Combine these with a few pretty shells and your table will be dressed for the occasion. Ask everyone to wear tropical outfits.

In the summer, transform your backyard into an island paradise. It's even more challenging to have this party in the middle of winter. Get in a tropical mood with glasses of Caribbean Connection in front of a roaring fire in the fireplace. Pass a tray of Sesame Chicken Wings and Aloha Ham Bites. Later, when seated around the dining table, serve Mariner's Filo Roll-Ups, which are crunchy layers of filo wrapped around crab-stuffed fillets of sole. Oasis Coleslaw and slices of a mango-wheat bread complete the main part of the meal. For dessert, there's a coconut-pineapple Trade-Winds Cake to complete your imaginary dream trip to the tropics. Serves 6 people.

MAKE-AHEAD PLAN:

- **Trade-Winds Cake**—Make up to 24 hours ahead. Glaze and slice 3 hours before serving.
- **South-Seas Loaf**—Make up to 24 hours ahead for ease in slicing.
- **Mariner's Filo Roll-Ups**—Fill and roll up to 24 hours ahead; bake just before serving.
- **Oasis Coleslaw**—Prepare cabbage and fruit up to 24 hours ahead. Make dressing up to 24 hours ahead, but do not combine with salad until served.
- **Sesame Chicken Wings**—Make up to 24 hours ahead.
- **Aloha Ham Bites**—Make up to 24 hours ahead.
- **Caribbean Connection**—Combine juice, coconut syrup and liqueurs up to 24 hours ahead. Add banana and ice at serving time; puree in blender.

Short-Cuts:

- Serve only 1 appetizer.
- Substitute ham cubes dipped in sauce for Aloha Ham Bites.
- Purchase date-nut bread or orange bread instead of making South-Seas Loaf.
- Make a coconut cake from a cake mix.

From top to bottom: Caribbean Connection, page 116, Sesame Chicken Wings, page 116, fresh fruit, Aloha Ham Bites, page 117.

Caribbean Connection

Photo on page 115.

A blend of island flavors in a great liquid form.

2 cups pineapple juice
6 tablespoons cream of coconut syrup
6 tablespoons almond-flavored liqueur
1/4 cup orange-flavored liqueur
Orange wedges

Fresh pineapple wedges
Fresh strawberries
1 banana
1-1/2 cups crushed ice

In a 2-quart pitcher, combine pineapple juice, cream of coconut, almond liqueur and orange liqueur. *Complete now or make ahead.*

To complete now, skewer orange wedges, pineapple wedges and strawberries on 6-inch skewers; set aside. Pour juice mixture into a blender. Add banana and ice. Process until banana is pureed. Immediately pour into tall wine or champagne glasses. Place 1 skewer with fruit in each glass.

To make ahead, cover and refrigerate up to 24 hours. Skewer fruit on 6-inch skewers. Wrap in plastic wrap; refrigerate 6 to 8 hours. To serve, proceed as directed above. Makes 6 servings.

● ● ●

Sesame Chicken Wings

Photo on page 115.

These also make ideal cold snacks.

4 lbs. chicken wings
2/3 cup all-purpose flour
2 eggs, lightly beaten
2 tablespoons water
2/3 cup finely crushed round rich crackers
2/3 cup grated Parmesan cheese (2 oz.)

2/3 cup sesame seeds, toasted
2 tablespoons minced fresh parsley
1/2 teaspoon seasoned pepper
1 teaspoon seasoned salt
1/4 cup butter or margarine, melted

Remove and discard wing tips. Cut apart remaining portions of wings at joints. Pour flour into a small shallow dish. In another small shallow dish or saucer, beat eggs with water. In a small bowl, combine cracker crumbs, Parmesan cheese, sesame seeds, parsley, seasoned pepper and seasoned salt. Preheat oven to 375F (190C). Pour melted butter or margarine into a 13" x 9" baking pan. Roll chicken pieces in flour, then in egg mixture; then roll in crumb mixture. Arrange coated chicken in a single layer in butter in baking pan. Bake in preheated oven 45 minutes. *Complete now or make ahead.*

To complete now, immediately arrange hot wing pieces on a platter or serving plate. Or, drain on paper towels; cool slightly. Cover; refrigerate until chilled. Serve cold chicken wings on a platter or serving plate.

To make ahead, drain baked chicken pieces on paper towels; place in a container with a tight-fitting lid. Refrigerate up to 24 hours. Serve warm or cold. To warm, place in a 13" x 9" baking pan; heat at 375F (190C) 15 to 20 minutes. Serve as directed above. Makes 36 to 40 appetizers.

Aloha Ham Bites

Photo on page 115.

A memorable appetizer with flavor appeal.

1/2 cup chopped dried apricots	1-1/2 cups flaked coconut
1 cup pineapple juice	1/2 cup mayonnaise
1 tablespoon white-wine vinegar	2 cups ground cooked ham
1 tablespoon honey	1/4 cup finely chopped peanuts
About 3 drops hot-pepper sauce or to taste	1 teaspoon prepared mustard

In a small saucepan, combine apricots, pineapple juice, vinegar, honey and hot-pepper sauce. Bring to a boil; reduce heat. Cover and simmer 15 minutes. Pour into a blender or food processor fitted with a metal blade. Process until pureed. Pour puree into a small bowl; set aside. Pour coconut into a pie plate; set aside. In a medium bowl, combine mayonnaise, ham, peanuts and mustard. Shape into 1/2- to 3/4-inch balls. Dip balls in apricot sauce, then roll in coconut. *Complete now or make ahead.*

To complete now, arrange on a platter or serving plate. Refrigerate at least 2 hours to chill thoroughly; serve cold.

To make ahead, arrange in a single layer in a container with a tight-fitting lid. Refrigerate up to 24 hours. Serve as directed above. Makes 35 to 45 appetizers.

South-Seas Loaf

This slightly spongy, firm-textured loaf stays moist because of the mango.

3/4 cup whole-wheat flour	1/3 cup honey
3/4 cup all-purpose flour	3/4 cup whole-bran cereal
1/4 teaspoon salt	3/4 cup dairy sour cream
2 teaspoons baking powder	1 large ripe mango, peeled, pureed
1 teaspoon baking soda	1 teaspoon grated orange peel
2 eggs, lightly beaten	1/3 cup flaked coconut
2 tablespoons vegetable oil	

Grease a 9" x 5" loaf pan; set aside. Preheat oven to 350F (175C). In a large bowl, combine whole-wheat flour, all-purpose flour, salt, baking powder and baking soda. In a medium bowl, combine eggs, oil, honey, whole-bran cereal, sour cream, mango, orange peel and coconut. Add egg mixture to dry ingredients. Stir only enough to moisten. Spoon into greased pan; smooth top. Bake in preheated oven 40 to 45 minutes or until a wooden pick inserted in center comes out clean. Cool in pan on a wire rack 10 minutes. Turn out onto rack; cool completely. *Complete now or make ahead.*

To complete now, let bread stand about 2 hours. Slice bread; arrange on a platter or serving plate.

To make ahead, make up to 24 hours ahead. Wrap cooled bread airtight with foil or plastic wrap. Let stand at room temperature up to 24 hours. Bread slices easier if made ahead. About 3 hours before serving, slice bread; arrange on a platter or serving plate. Cover with foil or plastic wrap; refrigerate until served. Makes 1 (9" x 5") loaf.

How to Make Mariner's Filo Roll-Ups

1/Spoon crabmeat mixture onto centers of sole fillets. Fold ends over filling, overlapping ends.

2/Fold sides of filo over stuffed fillet. Fold ends of filo over top, overlapping.

Mariner's Filo Roll-Ups

Crunchy and golden on the outside with delicately flavored seafood inside.

**About 6 oz. cooked, flaked crabmeat
(1 cup)**
1/2 cup chopped mushrooms
1 tablespoon minced fresh parsley
1/4 teaspoon dried dill weed
1/2 teaspoon salt

1/4 teaspoon pepper
1 cup soft bread crumbs
6 sole fillets
12 filo sheets
1/2 cup butter, melted

In a small bowl, combine crabmeat, mushrooms, parsley, dill weed, salt, pepper and bread crumbs. Spoon crabmeat mixture onto centers of sole fillets. Fold ends of fillets over filling, overlapping ends. Keep filo sheets covered until needed to prevent drying. Brush butter on 1 filo sheet. Top with a second filo sheet; brush with butter. Fold buttered filo sheets in half. Place 1 stuffed sole fillet in center of prepared filo. Fold long sides of filo over top, slightly overlapping. Fold ends over fillet, slightly overlapping. Place wrapped fillet, seam-side down, in an ungreased 13″ x 9″ baking dish. Brush with butter. Repeat with remaining fish fillets, filling and filo sheets. *Complete now or make ahead.*

To complete now, place in cold oven. Turn oven to 375F (190C). Bake 25 to 30 minutes or until filo is golden brown. Arrange baked roll-ups on a platter or serving dish; serve hot.

To make ahead, cover dish with foil or plastic wrap; refrigerate up to 24 hours. Bake and serve as directed above. Makes 6 servings.

Oasis Coleslaw

Irresistibly refreshing salad with a variety of flavors.

1/2 medium head cabbage, shredded
2 navel oranges, peeled, diced
1/2 cup chopped dates
1/2 cup dairy sour cream
1/4 teaspoon dry mustard

1 tablespoon honey
2 teaspoons minced crystallized ginger
1/2 teaspoon salt
1/8 teaspoon pepper

In a large bowl, combine cabbage, oranges and dates. In a small bowl, combine sour cream, mustard, honey, crystallized ginger, salt and pepper. *Complete now or make ahead.*

To complete now, pour dressing over cabbage mixture; toss to distribute. Spoon into a serving bowl.

To make ahead, cover cabbage mixture and sour-cream dressing with foil or plastic wrap. Refrigerate separately up to 24 hours. Serve as directed above. Makes 5 or 6 servings.

Trade-Winds Cake

Cream of coconut is a white, coconut-flavored syrup found in gourmet sections of supermarkets.

3 eggs
3/4 cup vegetable oil
1 cup sugar
1/2 cup cream of coconut
1 (8-oz.) can crushed pineapple in syrup
2 tablespoons almond-flavored liqueur
1 teaspoon grated orange peel

3 cups all-purpose flour
2 teaspoons baking powder
1 teaspoon baking soda
2 teaspoons cornstarch
2 tablespoons sugar
1/4 cup orange juice
1 tablespoon almond-flavored liqueur

Grease and flour a 10-inch tube pan; set aside. Preheat oven to 350F (175C). In a large bowl, beat eggs lightly. Add oil, 1 cup sugar and cream of coconut; beat until thick and foamy. Drain pineapple, reserving 1/2 cup syrup for glaze. To egg mixture, add drained pineapple, 2 tablespoons liqueur and orange peel. In a medium bowl, combine flour, baking powder and baking soda; stir into egg mixture. Pour batter into prepared pan. Bake in preheated oven 45 to 55 minutes or until a wooden pick inserted off center comes out clean. Let stand in pan 10 minutes. Invert onto a wire rack; remove pan. Cool completely. *Complete now or make ahead.*

To complete now, in a small saucepan, combine cornstarch, 2 tablespoons sugar, reserved pineapple syrup and orange juice. Stirring, cook until thickened. Stir in 1 tablespoon liqueur; cool 5 minutes. Spoon or brush warm glaze over cooled cake. Let stand until glaze sets. Slice; arrange on a platter or serving plate.

To make ahead, bake cake up to 24 hours ahead; wrap airtight. Prepare glaze; brush over cake 2 to 3 hours before serving. Cover to prevent drying. Makes 1 (10-inch) cake.

Mediterranean Flavors

Three-Way Gnocchi
Mediterranean-Style Lamb Kabobs
Make-Ahead Rice, page 105
Provençal Zucchini Bake
Rosy Raspberry Pears
Brie Cheese

Borrow favorite flavors from the well-known gastronomical areas of the Mediterranean to create your own fabulous dinner party. Follow the lead of chefs from world-famous restaurants by using fresh herbs and fresh produce whenever possible. For this special dinner, feature Mediterranean-Style Lamb Kabobs. They will give a wonderful fragrance to your house while cooking, in addition to mouthwatering goodness at your table.

Three-Way Gnocchi is a recipe for wonderful, light potato morsels topped with a choice of three sauces. It never fails to win admiration as an impressive first course to an elegant sit-down dinner.

We prefer to use fresh herbs in our dishes; however, some are in short supply during some times of the year. As a general rule, substitute about one-third or one-fourth the amount of dried herbs for their fresh counterparts. If you are unsure about the amount, taste whenever preparation of a dish is at a stage when sampling is feasible. Serves 6 to 8 people.

MAKE-AHEAD PLAN:

- **Three-Way Gnocchi**—Make gnocchi and sauces up to 24 hours ahead; divide among 3 baking dishes. Add a different topping to each dish; cover and refrigerate up to 24 hours. Bake during final 10 to 15 minutes that zucchini dish bakes.
- **Provençal Zucchini Bake**—Make up to 24 hours ahead. Bake zucchini before broiling meat.
- **Make-Ahead Rice**—Make up to 24 hours ahead; reheat about 10 minutes before serving.
- **Mediterranean-Style Lamb Kabobs**—Cover lamb with herbs; refrigerate up to 24 hours. Broil just before serving.
- **Rosy Raspberry Pears**—Make up to 24 hours ahead.

Short-Cuts:

- Serve steamed or sautéed zucchini instead of molded Provençal Zucchini Bake.
- Omit Three-Way Gnocchi.
- Use instant rice instead of Make-Ahead Rice.

Mediterranean-Style Lamb Kabobs

Just the right combination of flavors to bring out the best in lamb.

1 tablespoon chopped fresh thyme or
   1 teaspoon dried leaf thyme
1 tablespoon chopped fresh rosemary or
   1 teaspoon dried rosemary
1 garlic clove, crushed
1 teaspoon grated lemon peel
1 teaspoon salt

1/4 teaspoon pepper
2 teaspoons Dijon-style mustard
1/4 cup lemon juice
1/2 cup olive oil or vegetable oil
2-1/2 to 3 lbs. boned leg of lamb,
   cut in 1-1/2-inch cubes

In a shallow 10" x 6" baking dish, combine all ingredients except lamb. Add lamb, turning to coat all sides. Cover with foil or plastic wrap. *Complete now or make ahead.*

To complete now, refrigerate at least 2 hours. Drain, reserving marinade. Thread lamb cubes on 8 (10- or 12-inch) metal skewers. Place skewered meat on a broiler pan; brush with reserved marinade. Preheat broiler. Broil 4 to 5 inches from heat 3 to 4 minutes on each side, brushing with marinade. Arrange broiled kabobs on a platter or serving plate; serve hot.

To make ahead, refrigerate up to 24 hours. Broil as directed above. Makes 8 servings.

Provençal Zucchini Bake

Attractive zucchini dish makes an impressive visual effect.

6 to 8 medium zucchini, cut in 3/8-inch
   diagonal slices
2 teaspoons salt
1/4 cup vegetable oil
1 large onion, chopped
8 medium tomatoes, peeled, seeded, chopped
1 garlic clove, crushed

1/2 teaspoon dried leaf basil
1/4 teaspoon salt
1/8 teaspoon pepper
1/4 cup beef broth or bouillon
1/2 pint dairy sour cream (1 cup)
1 egg, lightly beaten
1/2 cup grated Parmesan cheese (1-1/2 oz.)

Sprinkle zucchini with salt. Place in a colander; let stand 2 hours. Rinse; drain and pat dry with paper towels. In a large skillet, heat oil; add zucchini. Cook over medium heat about 5 minutes. Drain on paper towels. Add onion to skillet; sauté until golden. Stir in tomatoes, garlic, basil, salt and pepper. Stir over very low heat 30 to 40 minutes or until thick. Spoon 1 cup thickened tomato mixture into a small bowl. Stir in broth or bouillon. Reserve remaining tomato sauce. In another small bowl, combine sour cream and egg; set aside. Overlap slices of cooked zucchini on bottom and around side of a 1-quart charlotte mold or similar mold. Top with about 3 tablespoons tomato-broth mixture, 1/3 of sour-cream mixture and 1/3 of Parmesan cheese. Continue layering zucchini, tomato-broth mixture, sour-cream mixture and Parmesan cheese, ending with zucchini. Cover filled mold with foil. *Complete now or make ahead.*

To complete now, place covered mold in cold oven. Turn oven to 350F (175C). Bake 45 to 50 minutes. In a small saucepan, heat reserved tomato sauce. Pour into a serving bowl; keep hot. Invert mold onto a platter or serving plate; remove mold. Serve heated sauce separately.

To make ahead, refrigerate covered mold and reserved tomato sauce separately up to 24 hours. To bake, place covered mold in a cold oven; turn oven to 350F (175C). Bake 55 to 60 minutes. Remove from oven; let stand 10 minutes. Heat reserved tomato sauce; serve as directed above. Makes 6 to 8 servings.

Three-Way Gnocchi

These versatile little morsels melt in your mouth.

6 medium baking potatoes
1 teaspoon salt

Gorgonzola Topping:
2 tablespoons grated Parmesan cheese
2 oz. Gorgonzola cheese, crumbled

Almond-Brie Topping:
2 oz. Brie cheese, cubed
1/4 cup half and half

Pesto Topping:
1 medium tomato, peeled, seeded, chopped
1/4 cup chopped fresh basil leaves or
  1/2 teaspoon dried leaf basil
1/4 cup ricotta cheese
1 garlic clove, crushed

1-1/4 to 1-1/2 cups all-purpose flour
1/4 cup butter or margarine, melted

2 tablespoons half and half
2 teaspoons minced fresh parsley

2 tablespoons sliced almonds

2 tablespoons chopped pine nuts
1/4 teaspoon salt
2 tablespoons grated Parmesan cheese
Basil sprig

Preheat oven to 400F (205C). Bake potatoes in preheated oven about 45 minutes or until tender. Peel cooked potatoes. Press peeled potatoes through a food ricer or mash with a potato masher. In a large bowl, combine mashed potatoes and salt. Gradually stir in enough flour to make a stiff dough. Turn out onto a lightly floured surface. Knead lightly, working in enough flour to make dough smooth and pliable. Divide dough into pieces about the size of an egg. Shape each piece into a 1/2-inch-thick log; cut each log into 1-inch lengths. Using tines of a fork, make light crosswise depressions in each 1-inch length. In a 4-quart pot, bring 3 quarts lightly salted water to a boil. Pour butter or margarine into a 13'' x 9'' baking pan. Carefully add about 1/4 of gnocchi to boiling water. After gnocchi float to top of water, cook 10 seconds. Use a slotted spoon to remove cooked gnocchi from boiling water; drain briefly. Stir into butter or margarine, coating all sides. Spoon coated cooked gnocchi evenly into 3 shallow medium casserole dishes or au gratin dishes; set aside. Prepare toppings.

To make Gorgonzola Topping, in a small bowl, combine Parmesan cheese, Gorgonzola cheese, half and half and 1 teaspoon minced parsley. Spread over gnocchi first of dishes.

To make Almond-Brie Topping, sprinkle Brie over gnocchi in second dish. Pour half and half over top. Sprinkle with almonds.

To make Pesto Topping, in a blender or food processor fitted with a metal blade, combine all pesto ingredients except basil sprig. Process until finely chopped but not pureed. Pour over gnocchi in remaining dish. *Complete now or make ahead.*

To complete now, cover dishes with foil; place in cold oven. Turn oven to 350F (175C). Bake 15 to 20 minutes or until bubbly; garnish Pesto Topping with basil sprig. Garnish Gorgonzola Topping with remaining teaspoon minced parsley. Serve hot in casserole or au gratin dishes.

To make ahead, cover prepared dishes with foil. Refrigerate up to 24 hours. To serve, place covered dishes in cold oven. Turn oven to 350F (175C). Bake 20 to 25 minutes or until bubbly. Garnish as directed above. Makes 6 to 8 servings.

How to Make Three-Way Gnocchi

1/Divide potato dough into egg-size pieces. Shape into logs; cut in 1-inch pieces.

2/Serve cooked gnocchi with sauces. Garnish each with appropriate garnish.

Rosy Raspberry Pears

Fruit juice gives a pretty pink color to this refreshing pear dessert.

3 cups raspberry-cranberry-juice drink
1 (3-inch) cinnamon stick
4 whole cloves
1/4 cup sugar

2 unpeeled lemon slices
4 large ripe pears
1/4 cup black-raspberry liqueur

In a 10-inch skillet, combine juice drink, cinnamon, cloves, sugar and lemon slices. Bring to a boil. Peel, halve and core pears. Using a slotted spoon, carefully lower peeled pear halves into boiling liquid. Cover skillet; simmer 8 to 10 minutes or until pears are tender when pierced with a fork. Remove from heat; stir in liqueur. Use a slotted spoon to place pears in a large bowl; pour hot juice over top. Cover with plastic wrap. *Complete now or make ahead.*

To complete now, refrigerate at least 2 hours. To serve, spoon pears and juice into individual dessert dishes.

To make ahead, refrigerate up to 24 hours. Serve as directed above. Makes 4 servings.

Chocoholics' Splurge

Chocolate-Hazelnut Dream
Triple-Chocolate Cheesecake
Fudge-Ribbon-Mousse Cake
Chocolate-Macadamia Tart
Peanut-Butter-Fudge Bars
Easy Fudge-Nut Truffles

*A*ttention, Chocoholics! If your idea of heaven is sampling five or six divine chocolate desserts, we have a plan for you! Stage an all-chocolate-dessert party. You don't need an excuse. Just invite 10 or 12 friends who are dedicated chocolate lovers. You can make-ahead all of our melt-in-your-mouth creations, then have time to enjoy them with your friends. We suggest you arrange the desserts buffet-style on your dining table. Cut each into small servings so guests won't feel guilty about sampling each. Offer coffee and tea for a change in flavor.

We'll guarantee you'll have requests for recipes from the most discriminating chocoholics. Serves 10 to 12 people.

MAKE-AHEAD PLAN:

- **Peanut-Butter-Fudge Bars**—Make and freeze up to 2 months ahead.
- **Chocolate-Hazelnut Dream**—Bake cake up to 1 month ahead. Freeze until day before your party. Make hazelnut filling up to 24 hours ahead. Fill and glaze cake early on day of party.
- **Fudge-Ribbon-Mousse Cake**—Bake cake up to 1 month ahead. Freeze until day before your party. Make mousse up to 24 hours ahead. It takes several hours to put this together so allow adequate time.
- **Easy Fudge-Nut Truffles**—Make and freeze up to 1 month ahead. Or, make and refrigerate up to 4 days.
- **Triple-Chocolate-Swirl Cheesecake**—Best when made 24 hours ahead. Allow enough time for baking, cooling and topping.
- **Chocolate-Macadamia Tart**—Best when made on day it's served, but may be made up to 24 hours ahead. Store in refrigerator.

Short-Cuts:

- Purchase a chocolate cake or cheesecake at a specialty bakery to substitute for 1 or more of our recipes.
- Use a brownie mix or bar-cookie mix for base of Peanut-Butter-Fudge Bars.
- Purchase truffles at your favorite candy store.

Fudge-Ribbon-Mousse Cake   *Photo on page 124.*

This melt-in-your-mouth, two-flavored mousse sits on a rich chocolate base.

2 eggs
1 cup sugar
1/2 cup butter or margarine, melted
3/4 cup all-purpose flour
1/4 cup unsweetened cocoa powder, sifted

1/2 teaspoon vanilla extract
3 oz. semisweet chocolate
Whipped cream, if desired
Chocolate curls and slivers, if desired

Ribbon Mousse:
1 (1/4-oz.) envelope unflavored gelatin
   (1 tablespoon)
1 cup milk
4 egg yolks
3/4 cup sugar

1 teaspoon vanilla extract
3 egg whites
1/4 cup sugar
1/2 pint whipping cream (1 cup)

Preheat oven to 350F (175C). Grease a 9-inch springform pan; set aside. In a medium bowl, beat 2 eggs until thick, about 5 minutes. Gradually beat in sugar. Stir in butter or margarine, flour, cocoa powder and vanilla. Pour into greased pan; bake in preheated oven 25 to 30 minutes or until cake begins to come away from edge of pan. Cool in pan on a wire rack. *Complete now or make ahead.*

To complete now, prepare Ribbon Mousse. Spoon 1/2 of white mousse mixture over cooled cake in springform pan; keep remaining half cool, but do not refrigerate. Refrigerate cake in springform pan about 1 hour or until mousse is firm. Melt chocolate over hot water; set aside to cool slightly. Stir slightly cooled chocolate into reserved 1/2 of mousse mixture; spoon over firm mixture in springform pan. Cover with foil or plastic wrap; refrigerate at least 4 hours. Remove side of springform pan. Using a wide spatula, lift cake from pan to a large round plate. Garnish with whipped cream and chocolate curls or slivers, if desired. Refrigerate until served. To serve, cut in thin wedges.

To make Ribbon Mousse, in a medium saucepan, sprinkle gelatin over milk; let stand 5 minutes. In a medium bowl, beat egg yolks and 3/4 cup sugar until thick, about 5 minutes. Stir egg-yolk mixture into milk mixture. Stirring constantly, cook over low heat until thickened. Remove from heat; stir in vanilla. Cool slightly; refrigerate about 1 hour or until mixture begins to set, stirring once. In a medium bowl, beat egg whites until foamy; beat in 1/4 cup sugar until stiff but not dry. In another medium bowl, beat 1 cup whipping cream until soft peaks form. Fold beaten egg whites into whipped cream. Fold whipped-cream mixture into chilled egg-yolk mixture.

To make ahead, bake cake up to 1 month ahead. Wrap airtight in freezer wrap or heavy foil; freeze. At least 24 hours before party, make and add mousse layers as directed above. Early on day of party, remove side of springform pan. Using a wide spatula, lift cake from pan to a large round plate. Garnish with whipped cream and chocolate curls or slivers, if desired. Refrigerate until served. Serve as directed above. Makes 8 to 10 servings.

Chocolate-Hazelnut Dream

Rich chocolate cake filled with a thick layer of hazelnuts and glazed with chocolate!

4 eggs
3/4 cup sugar
1/2 teaspoon vanilla extract

2/3 cup all-purpose flour
1/2 cup unsweetened cocoa powder
1/4 cup butter, melted

Hazelnut-Butter Filling:
2 cups hazelnuts
1/4 cup light corn syrup

1/4 cup butter, room temperature
1 cup sifted powdered sugar

Satiny Chocolate Glaze:
6 oz. semisweet chocolate
2 teaspoons vegetable oil

1/4 cup butter, room temperature

Grease and flour a round 9-inch cake pan; set aside. Preheat oven to 375F (190C). In a large bowl, beat eggs, sugar and vanilla until thick, about 5 minutes. Combine flour and cocoa powder in a sifter. Sift about 1/3 of flour mixture at a time into egg mixture; fold in after each addition. Carefully fold in butter. Spoon batter into prepared pan. Bake in preheated oven 25 to 30 minutes or until a wooden pick inserted in center comes out clean. Cool in pan on a wire rack 5 minutes. Invert onto rack; remove pan. Cool completely on rack. *Complete now or make ahead.*

To complete now, prepare Hazelnut-Butter Filling and Satiny Chocolate Glaze. Split cake layer in half horizontally. Place 1 cake layer, cut-side up, on a cake plate. Spread with filling. Top with remaining layer, cut-side down. Pour glaze over top of cake, letting excess glaze drip down sides. Let stand until glaze sets, at least 15 minutes. To serve, cut in wedges.

To make Hazelnut-Butter Filling, preheat oven to 400F (205C). Spread hazelnuts in a single layer in a 13" x 9" baking pan. Roast in preheated oven 5 to 8 minutes or until skins crack. Pour hot nuts onto center of a clean dish towel. Fold towel over nuts; rub briskly to remove most of skins. Discard skins. Pour skinned nuts into a blender or food processor fitted with a metal blade. Process until nuts are the consistency of peanut butter. Add corn syrup; process until blended. In a medium bowl, beat butter and powdered sugar until light and fluffy. Stir in hazelnut mixture until blended.

To make Satiny Chocolate Glaze, in a small heavy saucepan, combine chocolate, oil and butter. Stir constantly over low heat until chocolate melts.

To make ahead, bake cake up to 1 month ahead. Wrap in freezer wrap or heavy foil; freeze. Make hazelnut filling up to 24 hours ahead. Make glaze just before using. Split, fill and glaze cake. Serve as directed above. Makes 1 (9-inch) cake.

Triple-Chocolate Cheesecake

A real show-stopper!

1-3/4 cups chocolate-cookie crumbs
   (about 30 thin chocolate wafers)
1 tablespoon sugar
2 tablespoons butter or margarine, melted
2 (8-oz.) pkgs. cream cheese,
   room temperature
8 oz. cottage cheese (1 cup)
1-1/4 cups sugar

3 eggs, lightly beaten
1 teaspoon vanilla extract
1/2 pint whipping cream (1 cup)
1/2 cup unsweetened cocoa powder, sifted
1/2 teaspoon ground cinnamon
1/2 pint dairy sour cream (1 cup)
2 tablespoons sugar

Chocolate Leaves:
1 oz. semisweet chocolate

In a small bowl, combine cookie crumbs, 1 tablespoon sugar and butter or margarine. Press over bottom and about 1-1/2 inches up side of a 9-inch springform pan. Refrigerate while making filling. Preheat oven to 350F (175C). In a large bowl, combine cream cheese, cottage cheese and sugar; beat until smooth. Beat in eggs and vanilla. In a medium bowl, whip cream until soft peaks form; fold into cheese mixture. Spoon about 1/2 of filling into crumb-lined pan. Stir cocoa powder and cinnamon into remaining cheese mixture. Drop by large spoonfuls in 5 or 6 mounds on top of plain cheese filling in pan. Carefully pull broad side of a small spatula or table knife through both fillings several times in a zigzag pattern, being careful not to disturb crumb crust. Bake in preheated oven 65 to 70 minutes or until firm around edge and center jiggles slightly. Center will set up as it cools. Turn off oven heat; leave cheesecake in oven with door ajar 1 hour. Refrigerate at least 2 hours. *Complete now or make ahead.*

To complete now, prepare Chocolate Leaves. In a small bowl, combine sour cream and 2 tablespoons sugar. Spread sour-cream mixture over cooled cheesecake. Arrange chocolate leaves in a circle on center of cake. Refrigerate until served. To serve, cut in wedges.

To make Chocolate Leaves, select several unblemished non-poisonous leaves, such as rose or geranium leaves. Rinse and pat dry with paper towels. In a small bowl, melt chocolate over hot water. Use a small metal spatula or brush to spread melted chocolate about 1/8 inch thick over back side of leaves, just to edge. Carefully arrange on a flat pan or tray, chocolate-side up; refrigerate until firm. Carefully peel leaves away from chocolate.

To make ahead, bake crust and cheese filling up to 1 month ahead. Wrap airtight in freezer wrap or heavy foil; freeze. Thaw overnight in refrigerator. Add sour-cream mixture and leaf decoration 24 hours ahead or early on day of party. Serve as directed above. Makes 8 to 10 servings.

How to Make Triple-Chocolate Cheesecake

1/Spoon chocolate filling in mounds over white filling. Use a small spatula to swirl through.

2/Top baked cheesecake with sour-cream mixture. Garnish with chocolate leaves.

Peanut-Butter-Fudge Bars

A popular combination that says "love at first taste."

1/2 cup butter or margarine,
   room temperature
1/2 cup lightly packed brown sugar
1/2 teaspoon vanilla extract
1-1/2 cups all-purpose flour
1/2 cup chunk-style peanut butter,
   room temperature

1 cup semisweet chocolate pieces (6 oz.)
2 tablespoons milk
2 tablespoons light corn syrup
1/2 cup chopped peanuts

Preheat oven to 350F (175C). In a medium bowl, beat butter or margarine and brown sugar until creamy. Stir in vanilla and flour. Press over bottom of a 13″ x 9″ baking pan. Bake in preheated oven 15 to 20 minutes or until firm. Remove from oven; quickly spread peanut butter over top. In a small saucepan, combine chocolate pieces, milk and corn syrup. Stir constantly over low heat until chocolate melts. Spread over peanut butter. Sprinkle with peanuts. Cool in pan. *Complete now or make ahead.*

To complete now, cut into bars; arrange on a platter.

To make ahead, bake 3 or 4 days ahead. Cover with foil or plastic wrap; refrigerate. Or, bake up to 2 months ahead. Wrap in freezer wrap or heavy foil; freeze. Thaw at room temperature. Cut and serve as directed above. Makes 40 to 48 bars.

Chocolate-Macadamia Tart

One of our favorites—simply heavenly!

1 cup all-purpose flour
1/2 teaspoon salt
1/3 cup vegetable shortening

3 to 4 tablespoons water
1 oz. semisweet chocolate

Filling:
1 cup macadamia nuts
3 eggs, lightly beaten
3/4 cup light corn syrup

1/4 cup butter or margarine, melted
3/4 cup lightly packed brown sugar
1/2 teaspoon vanilla extract

In a medium bowl, combine flour and salt. Using a pastry blender or 2 knives, cut in shortening until mixture resembles coarse crumbs. Gradually stir in water until mixture forms a ball and comes away from side of bowl. On a lightly floured surface, roll out dough to an 11-inch circle, 1/8 inch thick. Use to line a 9-inch tart or quiche pan. Trim edges even with rim of pan; refrigerate. Preheat oven to 375F (190C). Prepare Filling. Spoon Filling into pastry-lined pan. Bake in preheated oven 35 to 40 minutes or until a wooden pick inserted in center comes out clean and filling is firm in center. If pie crust browns too quickly, cover edges with foil. Cool on a wire rack to room temperature. Melt chocolate over hot water or in a microwave. Drizzle over top of tart. *Complete now or make ahead.*

To make Filling, halve or quarter macadamia nuts with a knife, or coarsely chop in a food processor fitted with a metal blade. In a large bowl, combine eggs, corn syrup, butter or margarine, brown sugar and vanilla; beat until blended. Stir in chopped nuts.

To complete now, cut in wedges; serve immediately.

To make ahead, refrigerate completed tart up to 24 hours. Serve as directed above. Makes 1 (9-inch) tart.

• ● •

Easy Fudge-Nut Truffles

A magical concoction that's similar to other truffles, but takes less time to make.

1 (12-oz.) pkg. semisweet chocolate pieces
  (2 cups)
3/4 cup sweetened condensed milk

1 teaspoon vanilla extract
1 cup finely chopped walnuts or pecans

In top of a double boiler, melt chocolate pieces over hot water. Stir in condensed milk and vanilla. Spoon into a small shallow dish; refrigerate 10 to 15 minutes or until firm enough to shape. Place nuts in a pie plate. With a teaspoon, scoop chilled chocolate mixture; with another teaspoon, push mixture from spoon into nuts. Quickly roll in nuts, shaping into a rough ball. Place in a small bon-bon cup. Repeat with remaining chocolate mixture and nuts. Quickly arrange on a tray; refrigerate. *Complete now or make ahead.*

To complete now, refrigerate 15 minutes; arrange on a small platter or serving plate.

To make ahead, cover with foil or plastic wrap; refrigerate up to 4 days. Or, place tray in freezer. When truffles are frozen, place in freezer bags; freeze up to 1 month. Thaw in refrigerator. Remove 15 minutes before serving. Serve as directed above. Makes 24 truffles.

Deli Razzle-Dazzle

Marinated Roast Beef
Mustard-Cream Mold
Sliced Cold Meats   Marcy's Beef Sticks
Hot Potato Salad   Garden Medley
Whole-Wheat Herb-Cheese Bread
Peppered Brioche Loaf   Butter
Prepared Mustards   Rhineland Relish
Pickled Beets & Cucumbers
Fruit & Cheese Tray
or
Apple-Strudel Ring

Thanks to great advancements in our markets and gourmet stores, we have an unbelievable choice of good quality ready-to-serve foods. Our Deli Razzle-Dazzle features these foods. It's designed to fit into your lifestyle. We've included recipes for all prepared dishes on the menu. Depending on your schedule, we assume you'll make some of the foods and find it more convenient to purchase others.

Set your table as a buffet for six to eight people. With so many dishes in one meal, the food can be stretched to serve more. Serves 6 to 8 people.

MAKE-AHEAD PLAN:

- **Marcy's Beef Sticks**—Make and freeze up to 3 months ahead; thaw in refrigerator.
- **Whole-Wheat Herb-Cheese Bread**—Make; freeze up to 1 month. Or, refrigerate up to 2 days.
- **Peppered Brioche Loaf**—Make; freeze up to 1 month. Or, refrigerate up to 2 days.
- **Apple-Strudel Ring**—Bake; freeze up to 3 weeks. Or make 24 hours ahead.
- **Mustard-Cream Mold**—Make up to 24 hours ahead.
- **Rhineland Relish**—Make up to 24 hours ahead.
- **Marinated Roast Beef**—Marinate up to 24 hours.
- **Pickled Beets & Cucumbers**—Make up to 24 hours ahead.
- **Garden Medley**—Marinate up to 24 hours.
- **Hot Potato Salad**—Cook potatoes and bacon and prepare dressing up to 24 hours ahead.

Short-Cuts:

- Purchase bread, dessert and specialty mustards.

On following pages, clockwise from right: Peppered Brioche Loaf, page 137, Pickled Beets & Cucumbers, page 138, Rhineland Relish, page 135, Mustard-Cream Mold with assorted meats and cheeses, page 135, Hot Potato Salad, page 134, Garden Medley, page 136.

Marinated Roast Beef

The marinade is spicy, but not overpowering.

3/4 cup olive oil or vegetable oil
1/4 cup tarragon vinegar
1 tablespoon chopped watercress leaves
1 tablespoon chopped parsley
1 teaspoon Dijon-style mustard
1 teaspoon prepared horseradish

2 tablespoons capers, drained
1/2 teaspoon salt
1/4 teaspoon coarsely ground pepper
1 lb. rare roast beef, thinly sliced
1 red onion, thinly sliced

In a small bowl, combine oil, vinegar, watercress, parsley, mustard, horseradish, capers, salt and pepper. Place beef in a firm plastic container with a tight-fitting lid. Top with onion. Pour marinade over beef and onion. Cover with foil or plastic wrap. *Complete now or make ahead.*

To complete now, refrigerate 3 to 4 hours. Drain off and discard about 1/2 of marinade; arrange meat and onion on a platter or serving plate with a rim or sloping sides to keep marinade contained. Pour reserved marinade over meat and onion. Serve cold.

To make ahead, refrigerate up to 24 hours; serve as directed above. Makes about 6 servings.

Hot Potato Salad   *Photo on pages 132-133.*

The perfect accompaniment to deli meats.

6 large boiling potatoes
4 bacon slices, chopped
1 onion, chopped
1/4 cup all-purpose flour
2 tablespoons sugar
4 teaspoons Dijon-style mustard
1 tablespoon lemon juice

3 tablespoons white-wine vinegar
3/4 teaspoon salt
1/8 teaspoon pepper
1 cup water
1/4 teaspoon celery seeds
2 hard-cooked eggs, sliced

Cook potatoes in lightly salted water until tender but not overdone. When cool enough to handle, peel cooked potatoes; cut into 1/2-inch cubes. Place cubed potatoes in a large bowl; keep warm. Meanwhile, in a medium skillet, cook bacon until crisp; drain on paper towels. Reserve drippings in skillet. Crumble drained bacon; set aside. In hot bacon drippings, sauté onion until soft. Stir in flour and sugar until blended. Stir in mustard, lemon juice, vinegar, salt, pepper, water and celery seeds. Stirring constantly, cook over medium heat 2 to 3 minutes until thickened. *Complete now or make ahead.*

To complete now, pour vinegar mixture over cubed potatoes; toss to distribute. Spoon into a large salad bowl. Garnish with crumbled bacon and egg slices; serve hot.

To make ahead, cook, peel and cube potatoes 24 hours ahead. Place in a large bowl; cover with foil or plastic wrap. Refrigerate up to 24 hours. Cook, drain and crumble bacon; refrigerate in a small plastic bag up to 24 hours. Prepare dressing as directed above. Pour into a small bowl. Cover with foil or plastic wrap; refrigerate up to 24 hours. To serve, combine potatoes and dressing in a large skillet. Stir over low heat until heated through. Garnish and serve as directed above. Makes 6 servings.

Mustard-Cream Mold

Photo on pages 132-133.

Horseradish and mustard bring out the best in robust or mild-flavored meats.

1/2 cup sugar
1 (1/4-oz.) envelope unflavored gelatin
  (1 tablespoon)
1/2 cup white-wine vinegar
1 cup water
2 eggs, lightly beaten
2 tablespoons Dijon-style mustard
1 tablespoon prepared horseradish

1/2 teaspoon grated onion
1/2 pint dairy sour cream (1 cup)
Curly lettuce leaves
Endive
Pimento-stuffed green-olive slices
Assorted sliced cold meats
Assorted sliced cheeses

In a medium saucepan, combine sugar and gelatin. Add vinegar and water. Stir constantly over medium heat until sugar dissolves. Remove from heat. Stir about 1/2 cup hot mixture into eggs. Stir egg mixture into remaining hot mixture in pan. Stirring constantly, cook over low heat until thickened. Remove from heat. Stir in mustard, horseradish, onion and sour cream. Pour into a 4-cup mold. Cover with foil or plastic wrap. *Complete now or make ahead.*

To complete now, refrigerate at least 4 hours. Line a large platter or serving plate with lettuce leaves. Invert molded mixture onto lettuce-lined platter or plate; remove mold. Garnish top of mold with endive and green-olive slices. Arrange sliced cold meats and cheeses around molded mixture. Serve immediately.

To make ahead, refrigerate up to 24 hours. Serve as directed above. Makes about 3 cups.

———————— • • ————————

Rhineland Relish

Photo on pages 132-133.

Serve with deli meats.

1 small green bell pepper, finely chopped
1 small onion, finely chopped
3/4 cup vinegar
1 cup sugar

1/2 teaspoon mustard seeds
1/4 teaspoon celery seeds
2 cups sauerkraut

In a medium bowl, combine green pepper and onion; set aside. In small a saucepan, combine vinegar, sugar, mustard seeds and celery seeds. Bring to a boil. Pour hot syrup over green pepper and onion. Rinse and drain sauerkraut. Add to green-pepper mixture. Cover with foil or plastic wrap. *Complete now or make ahead.*

To complete now, refrigerate at least 4 hours. Drain; spoon into a serving dish. Serve as a relish.

To make ahead, refrigerate up to 24 hours. Drain and serve as directed above. Makes about 2 cups.

Whole-Wheat Herb-Cheese Bread

What a marvelous aroma and flavor!

1 (1/4-oz.) pkg. active dry yeast
   (1 tablespoon)
1/4 cup warm water (110F, 45C)
1 cup milk, room temperature
1 tablespoon sugar
2 tablespoons butter or margarine
1 teaspoon salt
1 tablespoon poppy seeds

1 tablespoon instant minced onion
2 teaspoons dried leaf marjoram
1/2 teaspoon ground sage
1-1/2 cups whole-wheat flour
1-1/2 to 2 cups all-purpose flour
4 oz. Cheddar cheese, cut in
   1/4-inch cubes (1 cup)

In a large bowl, sprinkle yeast over water. Let stand until yeast is softened. Stir in milk, sugar, butter or margarine, salt, poppy seeds, onion, marjoram, sage, whole-wheat flour and 1/2 cup all-purpose flour. Beat until smooth. Add enough remaining all-purpose flour to make a medium-stiff dough. Turn out on a lightly floured surface. Knead about 5 minutes or until smooth. Flatten dough with your hands. Sprinkle cheese cubes over dough; briefly knead in cheese cubes. Clean and grease bowl. Place kneaded dough in bowl, turning to grease all sides. Cover with a dry cloth; let rise in a warm place, free from drafts, until doubled in bulk, about 1-1/2 hours. Grease a 9″ x 5″ loaf pan. Punch down dough; shape into a loaf. Place into greased pan. Cover; let rise until nearly doubled in bulk, about 1 hour. Preheat oven to 375F (190C). Bake in preheated oven 30 minutes, covering with foil during last 5 minutes of baking. Remove from pan; cool loaf on a wire rack. *Complete now or make ahead.*

To complete now, let stand at room temperature 10 to 15 minutes. Slice bread; arrange on a platter or in a shallow bowl. Serve warm or at room temperature.

To make ahead, wrap cooled loaf in foil or plastic wrap; refrigerate up to 2 days. Or, wrap in freezer wrap; freeze up to 1 month. Thaw at room temperature. Slice and serve as directed above. Makes 1 loaf.

Garden Medley   *Photo on pages 132-133.*

Colorful fresh-vegetable combination.

2 yellow crookneck squash, thinly sliced
2 zucchini, thinly sliced
12 cherry tomatoes, halved
1/2 cup olive oil or vegetable oil
1/4 cup tarragon vinegar
1 tablespoon lemon juice
2 teaspoons Dijon-style mustard

1 tablespoon minced green onion
2 tablespoons minced watercress leaves
1/4 teaspoon dried leaf chervil
1/2 teaspoon salt
1/4 teaspoon pepper
Lettuce leaves

In a large bowl, combine crookneck squash, zucchini and tomatoes. In a small bowl, combine oil, vinegar, lemon juice, mustard, green onion, watercress, chervil, salt and pepper. Pour over vegetables; toss until well blended. Cover with foil or plastic wrap. *Complete now or make ahead.*

To complete now, refrigerate at least 2 hours. Line a serving bowl with lettuce leaves. Drain off most of marinade. Spoon drained vegetables into lettuce-lined bowl; serve cold.

To make ahead, refrigerate up to 24 hours. Drain and serve as directed above. Makes 6 servings.

Peppered Brioche Loaf

Photo on pages 132-133.

Two peppers join forces for a surprise loaf that's destined to be your favorite.

1 (1/4-oz.) pkg. active dry yeast
  (1 tablespoon)
1/2 cup warm water (110F, 45C)
3 eggs, lightly beaten
1/2 cup butter, cut into 8 pieces,
  room temperature
2 tablespoons sugar

1 teaspoon salt
3 to 3-1/2 cups all-purpose flour
1/2 teaspoon coarsely ground black pepper
1/2 teaspoon seasoned pepper
1 egg yolk, lightly beaten
1 teaspoon milk
Seasoned pepper, if desired

In a large bowl, sprinkle yeast over water. Let stand until yeast is softened. Stir in 3 eggs, butter, sugar, salt, yeast mixture and 1 cup flour. Beat with an electric mixer 2 minutes or beat with a whisk 5 minutes. Add black pepper and 1/2 teaspoon seasoned pepper. Gradually add enough remaining flour to make a dough that is shiny, pliable and soft. Shape into a ball. Turn out onto a lightly floured surface. Using as little flour as possible on the board, knead 7 or 8 minutes until dough is elastic. Clean and grease bowl. Place kneaded dough in bowl, turning to grease all sides. Cover with a dry cloth; let rise in a warm place, free from drafts, until doubled in bulk, about 1 hour. Punch down dough; let stand 5 minutes. Grease a 9" x 5" loaf pan. Shape dough into a smooth oval about 8 inches long. Place in greased pan. Cover with a dry cloth; let rise until doubled in bulk, about 45 minutes. Preheat oven to 375F (190C). In a small bowl, combine egg yolk and milk; brush mixture over top of loaf. Sprinkle with seasoned pepper, if desired. Bake 40 minutes or until loaf sounds hollow when tapped with your fingers. If crust becomes too brown, cover with foil during final 10 minutes of baking. Cool in pan 5 minutes. Remove from pan; cool loaf on a wire rack. *Complete now or make ahead.*

To complete now, let stand at room temperature 10 to 15 minutes. Slice bread; arrange on a platter or in a shallow bowl. Serve warm or at room temperature.

To make ahead, wrap cooled loaf in foil or plastic wrap; refrigerate up to 2 days. Or, wrap in freezer wrap; freeze up to 1 month. Thaw at room temperature. To serve, warm 15 minutes in a 350F (175C) oven, if desired. Slice and serve as directed above. Makes 1 loaf.

●●●

Marcy's Beef Sticks

Make your own smoked, spicy cold meats.

3 lbs. lean ground beef
1 tablespoon mustard seeds
1 tablespoon garlic salt

1 tablespoon coarsely ground pepper
1 teaspoon hickory-smoked salt
1 tablespoon salt

In a large bowl, combine all ingredients. Cover with foil or plastic wrap; refrigerate 1 to 2 days. Stir well once or twice each day. Shape into 3 rolls, each about 7 inches long and 2-1/2 inches thick. Place on a rack in a baking pan. Place in cold oven. Turn oven to 200F (95C). Bake 12 hours, turning beef rolls a quarter turn every 3 hours. Let cool completely on a wire rack; wrap airtight in foil or plastic wrap. *Complete now or make ahead.*

To complete now, refrigerate at least 2 hours. Cut into paper-thin crosswise slices. Serve on a platter or serving plate.

To make ahead, refrigerate up to 2 days. Or, wrap in freezer wrap; freeze up to 3 months. Thaw in refrigerator 6 to 8 hours. Serve as directed above. Makes 3 sticks or about 150 very thin slices.

Apple-Strudel Ring

Golden-brown flaky filo encases a wonderful apple-almond filling.

5 large cooking apples, cored, peeled,
   thinly sliced
1/4 cup granulated sugar
1/4 cup lightly packed brown sugar
1/2 teaspoon ground cinnamon
2 tablespoons lemon juice
1/4 cup golden raisins, chopped

1/2 cup chopped toasted almonds
1/2 cup vanilla-wafer crumbs
   (about 10 wafers)
1/2 cup butter, melted
6 filo-dough sheets
Powdered sugar
Whipped cream, if desired

In a medium bowl, combine apples, granulated sugar, brown sugar, cinnamon, lemon juice, raisins, almonds and 1/2 of vanilla-wafer crumbs; set aside. Reserve remaining crumbs. Brush a 9-inch ring mold with a little melted butter; set aside. Keep filo sheets covered to prevent drying. Working with 1 filo sheet at a time, brush 1 side of a filo sheet with butter; fold in half, buttered-sides together. Brush top of folded sheet with butter; fold in half again lengthwise. Brush top with butter. Ease into buttered mold, gently pressing filo over bottom, letting filo extend over side and center of mold. Repeat with remaining 5 filo sheets slightly overlapping where they extend over middle of mold, completely covering bottom and sides of mold. Sprinkle with reserved vanilla-wafer crumbs. Fill center with prepared apple mixture. Fold filo edges over apple mixture. Brush with melted butter. *Complete now or make ahead.*

To complete now, preheat oven to 375F (190C). Bake in preheated oven 40 minutes or until golden and crispy. To serve, invert onto a platter or serving plate; remove mold. Sprinkle with powdered sugar; cut into diagonal slices. Serve warm or at room temperature. Top with whipped cream, if desired.

To make ahead, cover with foil or plastic wrap; refrigerate up to 24 hours. Remove foil or plastic wrap; bake in preheated 375F (190C) oven 40 to 50 minutes or until golden and crispy. Or, immediately bake strudel ring; cool. Place in freezer until firm, about 4 hours. Remove from mold; wrap frozen strudel in heavy foil or place in a large freezer bag. Store in freezer up to 3 weeks. To serve frozen baked mold, return to original mold; thaw at room temperature. Preheat oven to 375F (190C). Place mold on a baking sheet. Heat 10 to 15 minutes or until warmed through. Remove from mold; slice. Serve as directed above. Makes 6 to 8 servings.

● ● ●

Pickled Beets & Cucumbers   *Photo on pages 132-133.*

An especially pleasing accompaniment to a pork roast.

1 (16-oz.) can sliced pickled beets, drained
1 cucumber, peeled, thinly sliced
2 tablespoons minced onion
1 teaspoon sugar
1/4 teaspoon salt

1/8 teaspoon pepper
1/4 teaspoon dried dill weed or
   1 teaspoon chopped fresh dill
1/2 cup dairy sour cream
Dill sprig

In a medium bowl, combine beets, cucumber, onion, sugar, salt, pepper and dill weed. Stir in sour cream. Cover with foil or plastic wrap. *Complete now or make ahead.*

To complete now, refrigerate at least 1 hour. Spoon into a serving bowl; garnish with dill sprig. Serve as a relish.

To make ahead, refrigerate up to 24 hours. Serve as directed above. Makes 6 servings.

How to Make Apple-Strudel Ring

1/Ease filo into mold. Gently press over bottom, letting filo extend over side and center of mold.

2/Sprinkle with reserved vanilla-wafer crumbs. Fill center with prepared apple mixture.

3/Fold filo edges over apple mixture; brush with melted butter. Bake 40 minutes or until golden.

4/Invert onto a platter; remove mold. Sprinkle with powdered sugar; cut into diagonal slices.

Salad Bonanza

Hearts o' Palm Salad
Executive-Suite Platter
Mustardy Vegetable Salad
Adriatic Summer Salad
Salmon Ring
Pacific-Shrimp Salad
Ranch-Relish Mold
Chinese-Chicken Salad Bowl
Old-South Loaf
Sourdough Bread   Butter
Spiced Island Cookies
Chocolate-Cheese Ribbons

*S*alad bars are everywhere—from very elegant restaurants to fast-food outlets. At home, you can expand this idea to create an exciting menu. Instead of having your guests make their own salads, make up six or seven different salads and set up a buffet. Let guests choose two or three salads or sample each one. Use your prettiest glass plates, salad bowls and platters to show off your culinary ability.

Although salads are the stars of the menu, one or two crunchy breads should be included. Old-South Loaf is slightly sweet, yet crunchy. It's an excellent contrast to all kinds of salads.

For those who are expecting dessert, set out a tray of Spiced Island Cookies and Chocolate-Cheese Ribbons. They are sure to satisfy the sweet tooth. Serves 10 to 12 people.

MAKE-AHEAD PLAN:

- **Spiced Island Cookies**—Make and freeze dough up to 1 month ahead. Or, refrigerate dough up to 2 weeks ahead. Bake up to 3 days ahead. Store at room temperature.
- **Old-South Loaf**—Make up to 5 days ahead; store in refrigerator.
- **Chocolate-Cheese Ribbons**—Make up to 24 hours ahead. Cover; store at room temperature.
- **Salmon Ring**—Make up to 24 hours ahead.
- **Ranch-Relish Mold**—Make up to 24 hours ahead. Unmold on a platter up to 3 hours ahead.
- **Hearts o' Palm Salad**—Make up to 24 hours ahead.
- **Pacific-Shrimp Salad**—Make up to 24 hours ahead.
- **Mustardy Vegetable Salad**—Make up to 24 hours ahead. Drain up to 1 hour before serving.
- **Adriatic Summer Salad**—Make up to 24 hours ahead.
- **Chinese-Chicken Salad Bowl**—Cook chicken and combine with sauce up to 24 hours ahead. Cook won-ton skins up to 24 hours ahead. Shred lettuce up to 4 hours ahead.

Short-Cuts:

- Omit 1 or 2 salads and 1 cookie. Buy cooked and shelled seafood. Invite fewer guests.

Chinese-Chicken Salad Bowl

Chicken skins get very crunchy and add richness to this dish.

4 boneless chicken-breast halves
2 tablespoons vegetable oil
1 tablespoon cornstarch
2 tablespoons soy sauce
1/4 cup hoisin sauce
1 cup chicken broth or bouillon
1/3 cup dry white wine
2 teaspoons sesame oil

1 (8-oz.) can water chestnuts, drained, chopped
1/4 cup chopped green onions
1 tablespoon minced gingerroot
1/2 cup vegetable oil
6 won-ton skins
1 small head lettuce
2 tablespoons toasted sesame seeds

Remove skin from chicken breasts; reserve skins. Heat 2 tablespoons oil in a large skillet. Add chicken breasts and skins; brown on both sides. Cook 15 minutes or until chicken is done and skins are crisp. Drain on paper towels; reserve drippings in pan. Cut cooled chicken and skin into julienne pieces; set aside. In a small bowl, stir cornstarch into soy sauce. Add cornstarch mixture, hoisin sauce, broth or bouillon, wine and sesame oil to pan. Stirring, cook over medium heat until translucent. Stir in cooked chicken and skin pieces, water chestnuts, green onions and gingerroot; set aside. Stack won-ton skins; cut in half horizontally, then vertically. Cut each square in half diagonally. Heat 1/2 cup oil in a medium skillet over medium-high heat. Fry won-ton pieces until golden; drain on paper towels. *Complete now or make ahead.*

To complete now, shred lettuce. In a large bowl, combine chicken mixture, shredded lettuce and fried won-ton skins. Sprinkle with sesame seeds. Serve cold.

To make ahead, spoon chicken mixture into a container with a tight-fitting lid. Refrigerate up to 24 hours. Place fried won-ton pieces in a plastic bag. Store at room temperature up to 24 hours. About 4 hours before serving, shred lettuce; refrigerate in a plastic bag. Serve in a large salad bowl as directed above. Makes 5 or 6 servings.

Hearts o' Palm Salad

A pure delight for starting that elegant dinner party.

2 tablespoons lemon juice
1/3 cup tarragon vinegar
1/2 cup olive oil or vegetable oil
2 garlic cloves, crushed
3 tablespoons minced watercress leaves
2 tablespoons minced pimento

2 teaspoons Dijon-style mustard
Salt and pepper to taste
1 (14-oz.) can whole hearts of palm, drained
1/2 lb. medium mushrooms, quartered
15 cherry tomatoes, halved
Lettuce leaves

In a small bowl, combine lemon juice, vinegar, oil, garlic, watercress, pimento, mustard, salt and pepper. Cut hearts of palm into 3/4-inch crosswise slices. In a large bowl, combine sliced hearts of palm, mushrooms and cherry tomatoes. Pour marinade over vegetables; toss lightly. *Complete now or make ahead.*

To complete now, marinate vegetables about 30 minutes. Line a salad bowl with lettuce. Spoon marinated vegetables into lettuce-lined bowl. Serve cold.

To make ahead, cover marinating vegetables with foil or plastic wrap; refrigerate up to 24 hours. Remove from refrigerator 20 to 30 minutes before serving. Serve as directed above. Makes 7 or 8 servings.

Adriatic Summer Salad

A special hot-weather treat when tomatoes and fresh basil are at their best.

4 tomatoes, sliced
1 red onion, thinly sliced
4 oz. mozzarella cheese, thinly sliced
1/2 cup coarsely chopped fresh basil
1/3 cup olive oil
1 tablespoon lemon juice
2 tablespoons red-wine vinegar

1 tablespoon minced parsley
1 garlic clove, crushed
1/2 teaspoon salt
1/4 teaspoon pepper
1/2 teaspoon Dijon-style mustard
1/2 cup sliced pitted ripe olives
Basil sprig

Arrange 1/2 of tomatoes, 1/2 of onion and 1/2 of mozzarella cheese in a large, shallow salad bowl. Sprinkle with 1/4 cup chopped basil. Top with remaining tomatoes, onion and cheese. In a small bowl, combine oil, lemon juice, vinegar, parsley, garlic, salt, pepper and mustard. Stir until blended. Pour over layered vegetables and cheese. Sprinkle with remaining 1/4 cup chopped basil. Cover with foil or plastic wrap. *Complete now or make ahead.*

To complete now, refrigerate at least 1 hour. Toss tomato mixture, distributing dressing. Sprinkle with olive slices; garnish with basil sprig.

To make ahead, refrigerate up to 24 hours. To serve, toss and garnish as directed above. Makes 6 servings.

Executive-Suite Platter

An intriguing combination for an extra-special salad.

1/4 cup olive oil or vegetable oil
1/4 cup tarragon vinegar
1/4 cup mayonnaise
1 teaspoon Dijon-style mustard
1 tablespoon lemon juice
1/4 teaspoon dried leaf chervil
1/2 teaspoon salt
1/4 teaspoon pepper

2 tablespoons minced green onions
1 tablespoon capers, drained
1 (14-oz.) can artichoke-heart halves
1/2 lb. mushrooms, thinly sliced
Boston- or Bibb-lettuce leaves
2 tomatoes, cut in wedges
2 ripe avocados, sliced
1/2 lb. shredded cooked crabmeat or lobster

In a blender or food processor fitted with a metal blade, combine oil, vinegar, mayonnaise, mustard, lemon juice, chervil, salt and pepper. Process until blended. Add green onions and capers; with quick on/off motions, process until blended. Pour into a medium bowl. Drain artichoke hearts; add to dressing. Add mushrooms; toss to coat. Cover with foil or plastic wrap. *Complete now or make ahead.*

To complete now, refrigerate at least 2 hours. Drain, reserving dressing. Arrange lettuce on a platter or serving plate. Spoon drained mushrooms and artichokes onto center of lettuce. Arrange tomato wedges and avocado slices around side. Top with crabmeat or lobster. Spoon reserved dressing over salad, or serve dressing separately.

To make ahead, refrigerate up to 24 hours. Remove from refrigerator 20 to 30 minutes before serving. Drain, reserving dressing. Serve as directed above. Makes 6 to 8 servings.

Ranch-Relish Mold

Adds a dash of color to your menu.

1/2 cup vinegar
1/2 cup sugar
2 cups water
1 tablespoon pickling spices
2 (1/4-oz.) envelopes unflavored gelatin
  (2 tablespoons)
1/2 cup cold water
1/2 cup dry white wine

1 (10-oz.) pkg. frozen whole-kernel corn or
  1 cup fresh corn, cooked, drained
1 cup finely shredded cabbage
2 tablespoons chopped green onions
1 tablespoon chopped pimento
Lettuce or other greens
Cherry-tomato halves
Celery leaves

In a medium saucepan, combine vinegar, sugar, 2 cups water and pickling spices. Bring to boil; simmer 5 minutes. Line a sieve with 2 layers of damp cheesecloth; place over a large bowl. Pour vinegar mixture through lined sieve to remove spices. In a small bowl, sprinkle gelatin over 1/2 cup cold water; stir to blend and soften. Add to hot vinegar mixture; stir until gelatin dissolves. Stir in wine. Refrigerate until mixture almost holds its shape when dropped from a spoon, 30 to 45 minutes. Stir in corn, cabbage, green onions and pimento. Spoon into an ungreased 6-cup mold; cover with foil or plastic wrap. *Complete now or make ahead.*

To complete now, refrigerate 4 hours or until firm. Arrange lettuce or other greens on a platter or serving plate. Invert mold onto lined platter or plate; remove mold. Garnish with cherry-tomato halves and celery leaves. Serve immediately.

To make ahead, refrigerate up to 24 hours. About 3 hours before serving, invert mold onto lined platter or plate; remove mold. Garnish as directed above. Refrigerate until served. Makes 5 or 6 servings.

Mustardy Vegetable Salad

Guaranteed to please even the most dedicated vegetable-hater.

2 cups cauliflowerets, cooked crisp-tender
  (1/2 medium head)
3 carrots, sliced, cooked crisp-tender
1-1/2 cups sliced mushrooms (about 1/4 lb.)
2 tablespoons butter or margarine
4 teaspoons all-purpose flour
1/2 cup sugar

1 tablespoon Dijon-style mustard
1/2 cup cider vinegar
1/2 teaspoon salt
1/8 teaspoon pepper
1 small onion, chopped
1 celery stalk, chopped

In a large bowl, combine cauliflowerets, carrots and mushrooms; set aside. In a small saucepan, melt butter or margarine; stir in flour. Stirring constantly, cook over medium heat 1 minute. Stir in sugar; then stir in mustard and vinegar. Continue stirring 2 minutes or until translucent and slightly thickened. Remove from heat. Stir in salt, pepper, onion and celery. Pour over vegetables; mix well. Cover with foil or plastic wrap. *Complete now or make ahead.*

To complete now, refrigerate at least 2 hours. Drain; spoon into a decorative salad bowl. Serve cold.

To make ahead, refrigerate up to 24 hours. Up to 1 hour before serving, drain. Serve as directed above. Makes 5 or 6 servings.

How to Make Ranch Relish Mold

1/Stir corn, cabbage, green onions and pimento into partially set gelatin mixture. Spoon into a 6-cup mold.

2/Invert mold onto a serving plate. Garnish with cherry-tomato halves and celery leaves.

Pacific-Shrimp Salad

A delightfully different hot-weather salad.

3 cups cold cooked long-grain white rice
1/2 lb. shelled cooked small shrimp
3 oranges or peaches, peeled, chopped
1 cup seedless grapes, halved
1/2 cup dairy sour cream
1/2 cup mayonnaise
1 teaspoon curry powder
1/4 teaspoon celery seeds

1/4 teaspoon salt
1/8 teaspoon pepper
2 tablespoons orange juice
1 tablespoon honey
1/4 cup toasted slivered almonds
Lettuce
1 small cantaloupe or honeydew melon,
  peeled, cut in wedges

Fluff rice; spoon into a 2-1/2-quart bowl. Top with shrimp, then oranges or peaches and grapes. In a small bowl, combine sour cream, mayonnaise, curry powder, celery seeds, salt, pepper, orange juice and honey. Stir until blended; pour over fruit. Sprinkle almonds over top; cover with foil or plastic wrap. *Complete now or make ahead.*

To complete now, refrigerate layered salad at least 2 hours. Toss to distribute ingredients. Line a platter or salad bowl with lettuce. Spoon salad onto lettuce; garnish with cantaloupe or honeydew melon. Serve immediately.

To make ahead, refrigerate salad up to 24 hours. About 1 hour before serving, toss to distribute ingredients. Spoon salad onto lettuce-lined plate or bowl; garnish as directed above. Refrigerate until served. Makes 6 to 8 servings.

Salmon Ring

Delicately flavored mold accented with bits of salmon.

1/4 cup dry white wine
2 (1/4-oz.) envelopes unflavored gelatin
   (2 tablespoons)
1 cup chicken broth or bouillon
1/3 cup chopped celery
2 green onions, chopped
1/2 teaspoon salt
2 tablespoons lemon juice

1/4 cup sweet-pickle relish, drained
1/2 teaspoon dried dill weed
1/4 cup dairy sour cream
1 (15-1/2-oz.) can salmon, drained, flaked
1/2 pint half and half (1 cup)
2 egg whites
Lettuce leaves
3 hard-cooked eggs, quartered

Pour wine into a small saucepan; sprinkle gelatin over wine. Let stand 3 to 4 minutes to soften; add broth or bouillon. Stir over very low heat 3 to 4 minutes until gelatin dissolves; set aside. In a blender or food processor fitted with a metal blade, combine celery, green onions, salt, lemon juice, pickle relish, dill weed and sour cream. Process until blended but not pureed. Add gelatin mixture, salmon and half and half. Process 2 to 5 seconds to break up salmon. In a large bowl, beat egg whites until stiff but not dry. Fold salmon mixture into beaten egg whites. Spoon into a 5-cup ring mold. Cover with foil or plastic wrap. *Complete now or make ahead.*

To complete now, refrigerate at least 4 hours. To serve, arrange lettuce leaves around edge of a medium, round platter or tray. Invert mold onto lettuce-lined platter or tray; remove ring mold. Arrange hard-cooked eggs around mold.

To make ahead, refrigerate up to 24 hours. Up to 3 hours before serving, invert mold onto lettuce-lined platter or tray; refrigerate. Garnish and serve as directed above. Makes 5 cups.

●●●

Old-South Loaf

Sweet potato joins forces with spices for a wonderful flavor surprise.

2 cups all-purpose flour
1/2 cup lightly packed brown sugar
1 teaspoon baking powder
1 teaspoon baking soda
1/4 teaspoon ground ginger
1/2 teaspoon ground nutmeg
1/2 teaspoon salt

1/4 cup vegetable oil
3/4 cup milk
2 eggs, lightly beaten
1 cup grated uncooked sweet potato
1 teaspoon grated orange peel
1/2 cup chopped pecans

Grease a 9" x 5" loaf pan; set aside. Preheat oven to 350F (175C). In a large bowl, combine flour, brown sugar, baking powder, baking soda, ginger, nutmeg, salt, oil, milk and eggs. Stir with a wooden spoon until blended. Stir in sweet potato, orange peel and pecans. Spoon into greased pan. Bake in preheated oven 60 to 65 minutes or until a wooden pick inserted in center comes out clean. Remove from pan; cool on a wire rack. Wrap cooled loaf in foil or plastic wrap. *Complete now or make ahead.*

To complete now, refrigerate about 2 hours. To serve, slice and arrange on a platter or serving plate.

To make ahead, store loaf up to 24 hours at room temperature or up to 5 days in refrigerator. Serve as directed above. Makes 1 loaf.

Chocolate-Cheese Ribbons

Chocolate pieces make it special.

1/2 cup butter, room temperature
3/4 cup sugar
1 egg
1 teaspoon vanilla extract
1/4 teaspoon baking soda
1-3/4 cups all-purpose flour
2 (3-oz.) pkgs. cream cheese,
 room temperature

1/3 cup sugar
2 tablespoons all-purpose flour
1 teaspoon vanilla extract
1/4 cup chopped walnuts
1/2 cup miniature semisweet chocolate pieces
1/2 teaspoon vegetable oil
1/4 cup semisweet chocolate pieces

In a medium bowl, beat butter and 3/4 cup sugar until fluffy. Beat in egg and 1 teaspoon vanilla; then beat in baking soda and 1-3/4 cups flour. Shape into 2 balls; wrap each in plastic wrap. Refrigerate at least 2 hours. To make filling, in a medium bowl, beat cream cheese until smooth. Beat in 1/3 cup sugar, 2 tablespoons flour and 1 teaspoon vanilla. Stir in walnuts and miniature chocolate pieces; set aside. Preheat oven to 350F (175C). Roll out 1 ball of dough to a 15″ x 5″ rectangle. Place on an ungreased baking sheet. Spread 1/2 of filling lengthwise on 1/2 of dough to within 1/2 inch of edge. Brush all edges with water; fold uncovered dough over filling. Press edges to seal. Repeat with remaining dough and filling. Bake in preheated oven 20 to 25 minutes or until light brown. Cool on baking sheet. Combine oil and 1/4 cup chocolate pieces in top of a double boiler over simmering water. Stir until smooth; drizzle over baked dough. When glaze sets, cut into 1-inch diagonal slices. *Complete now or make ahead.*

To complete now, arrange ribbons on a platter or serving plate. Serve at room temperature.

To make ahead, bake up to 24 hours ahead. Place slices in a single layer in a container with a tight-fitting lid; store at room temperature. Serve as directed above. Makes 30 slices.

Spiced Island Cookies

Crunchy and mildly spiced.

1 cup butter or margarine, room temperature
1 cup firmly packed brown sugar
2-1/2 cups all-purpose flour
1/4 teaspoon baking soda

1/2 teaspoon ground nutmeg
2 teaspoons ground cinnamon
1/4 cup dairy sour cream
1/2 cup coarsely chopped cashews

In a medium bowl, cream butter or margarine and brown sugar until fluffy. In another medium bowl, blend flour, baking soda, nutmeg and cinnamon. Add dry mixture alternately with sour cream to creamed mixture, beating until smooth after each addition. Stir in cashews. Divide dough in half; shape each half into a 2-inch-diameter roll. *Complete now or make ahead.*

To complete now, wrap in waxed paper; refrigerate 2 hours. Preheat oven to 350F (175C). Cut refrigerated dough into 1/4-inch slices. Place 2 inches apart, on an ungreased baking sheet. Bake 10 minutes. Remove from baking sheet; cool on a wire rack. Serve on a platter.

To make ahead, wrap dough rolls in waxed paper; place rolls in freezer bags; seal. Store in freezer up to 1 month. Or, refrigerate dough up to 2 weeks. Thaw frozen dough in refrigerator. Cut, bake and serve as directed above. Makes 40 to 45 cookies.

Ice-Cream Rally

Vanilla Ice Cream
Lemon-Ginger Sorbet
Chocolate Ice Cream
White-Chocolate Ice Cream
Licorice-Chip Ice Cream
Strawberry-Banana Frozen Yogurt
Melba Sauce   Peanut-Fudge Sauce
Marbled Maple Sauce
Orange-Pecan Topping
Tropics Fruit & Nut Mix
Cookies

No doubt you would find it difficult to name anyone who doesn't like ice cream. Then what better fare could be served to young and old at a social occasion? Certainly there are few better ways to win the adoration of the small fry in your life. Ice cream is no longer a seasonal treat. So why not rally your friends for ice cream? In fact, throwing an ice-cream rally is itself excuse enough for having a social gathering.

Our menu serves about 20 people, unless one or two of the flavors are more popular with your guests than other flavors. If feasible, provide for buffet service; serving themselves will double your guests' pleasure.

An hour or two before serving, set up the buffet service. To do this, place the frozen desserts, in their metal or plastic containers, in a large, deep pan or plastic box. Arrange them two inches apart and two inches from the sides of the pan or box. Fill space between the containers with alternate layers of ice cubes or crushed ice and salt. Use a ratio of two cups table salt for each six pounds of ice cubes, or 1-1/2 cups rock salt with each six pounds crushed ice. When not scooping frozen dessert, cover the pan or box with foil to help keep the temperature below freezing.

A word of caution! The temperature under the container of brine will be very low. Therefore, if it is going to be put directly on a surface that can be marred by extreme cold, first place a thick wooden cutting board or 1 inch of newspaper on the surface. The cutting board and newspaper can be hidden by covering them with foil or an attractive cloth. Serves about 20 people.

MAKE-AHEAD PLAN:

- **Peanut-Fudge Sauce**—Make up to 1 month ahead.
- **Tropics Fruit & Nut Mix, Marbled Maple Sauce and Orange-Pecan Topping**—Make up to 3 weeks ahead.
- If using your own ice cubes for freezing ice cream or keeping it frozen during rally, start making and storing cubes about 7 days ahead.
- **Frozen Desserts**—Beginning 4 days before your rally, make 1 or 2 frozen desserts each day. Store in metal or plastic containers in your home freezer.
- **Melba Sauce**—Make up to 3 days ahead.
- Up to 24 hours ahead, assemble individual dessert or sherbet dishes and spoons; utensils for scooping frozen desserts; and containers for serving sauces, toppings and cookies.

Short-Cuts:

- Except for specific flavors and dry toppings, purchase all or any part of the menu at your supermarket or ice-cream store.
- There are many dry toppings that can be made in a jiffy from commercial products, such as chopped Oreo® cookies, crushed M&M® candies, chopped chocolate-peanut-butter cups, semisweet or milk-chocolate pieces, peanut-butter-flavored pieces and granola.

Vanilla Ice Cream   *Photo on page 151.*

A creamy, smooth basic vanilla ice cream.

1-1/3 cups sugar
1 tablespoon cornstarch
1/4 teaspoon salt
3 cups whole milk

2 egg yolks
1 (5.33-oz.) can evaporated milk
1/2 pint whipping cream (1 cup)
1 tablespoon vanilla extract

In a medium saucepan, combine sugar, cornstarch and salt. Stir in whole milk. Stir over medium heat until mixture begins to simmer. Simmer 1 minute over low heat. In a small bowl, lightly beat egg yolks. Stir about 1 cup milk mixture into egg yolks; stir egg-yolk mixture into remaining milk mixture. Stirring constantly, cook over low heat 2 minutes or until slightly thickened. Stir in evaporated milk, cream and vanilla. Cool to room temperature. Pour into ice-cream canister. Freeze in ice-cream maker according to manufacturer's directions. *Complete now or make ahead.*

To complete now, store in home freezer 1 to 3 hours until mixture is firm. To serve, arrange in a large box with several other frozen desserts. Surround with ice and salt as directed on opposite page. Dip ice-cream dipper into cold water before scooping individual servings. Serve in small bowls or sherbet dishes.

To make ahead, store frozen ice cream in home freezer up to 4 days. Serve as directed above. Makes about 2 quarts.

Variation

Chocolate Ice Cream: Substitute whole eggs for egg yolks. Reduce vanilla extract to 1 teaspoon. Stir 3 ounces melted semisweet chocolate into warm egg-milk mixture. Complete as directed above.

White-Chocolate Ice Cream

Cocoa butter in white chocolate provides a delicate, mellow flavor.

1/2 lb. white chocolate
2 tablespoons butter
1 cup milk
5 egg yolks

1/4 cup sugar
1 tablespoon light corn syrup
1 pint whipping cream (2 cups)

Cut white chocolate into small pieces. In a 2-quart saucepan, combine chocolate, butter and milk. Stir constantly over *very* low heat until chocolate and butter melt; remove from heat. In a small bowl, beat egg yolks and sugar with an electric mixer about 5 minutes or until thick. Stir egg-yolk mixture and light corn syrup into chocolate mixture. Stirring constantly, cook over low heat 8 to 10 minutes until thickened and mixture coats a metal spoon. Remove from heat; stir in cream. Cool to room temperature. Pour into ice-cream canister. Freeze in ice-cream maker according to manufacturer's directions. *Complete now or make ahead.*

To complete now, store in home freezer 1 to 3 hours until mixture is firm. To serve, arrange in a large box with several other frozen desserts. Surround with ice and salt as directed on page 148. Dip ice-cream dipper into cold water before scooping individual servings. Serve in small bowls or sherbet dishes.

To make ahead, store frozen ice cream in home freezer up to 4 days. Serve as directed above. Makes about 2 quarts.

●●●

Lemon-Ginger Sorbet

A most refreshing sorbet and a delight for all ages.

2-1/2 cups water
1 cup sugar
1-1/2 teaspoons grated gingerroot

2/3 cup lemon juice
1 teaspoon grated lemon peel

In a medium saucepan, combine water and sugar. Stir constantly over low heat until sugar dissolves. Stir in gingerroot, lemon juice and lemon peel; cool to room temperature. Pour into ice-cream canister. Freeze in ice-cream maker according to manufacturer's directions. *Complete now or make ahead.*

To complete now, store in home freezer 1 to 3 hours until mixture is firm. To serve, arrange in a large box with several other frozen desserts. Surround with ice and salt as directed on page 148. Dip ice-cream dipper into cold water before scooping individual servings. Serve in small bowls or sherbet dishes.

To make ahead, store frozen sorbet in home freezer up to 4 days. Serve as directed above. Makes about 1 quart.

How to Serve an Ice-Cream Rally

1/Place ice-cream containers in a large plastic box or pan. Surround with ice.

2/Layer ice and salt around containers, page 148. Protect surface underneath with a board or newspaper.

3/Scoop ice cream into individual bowls. Serve sauces and dry toppings separately.

4/Vanilla Ice Cream, page 149, topped with Peanut-Fudge Sauce, page 154, whipped cream and dry toppings.

Licorice-Chip Ice Cream

Even non-licorice fans demand second helpings of this smooth and tasty dessert.

6 to 8 oz. hollow licorice-candy twists
3/4 cup sugar
1 tablespoon cornstarch
1/4 teaspoon salt
2 cups milk

1 pint half and half (2 cups)
2 egg yolks
1/2 pint whipping cream (1 cup)
1 teaspoon anise extract

Place licorice twists in freezer 2 hours before making ice cream. In a medium saucepan, combine sugar, cornstarch and salt; stir in milk and 1 cup half and half. Stirring constantly, cook over low heat about 5 minutes or until slightly thickened; remove from heat. In a small bowl, beat egg yolks. Gradually stir about 1 cup milk mixture into beaten egg yolks. Stir egg-yolk mixture into remaining milk mixture. Stirring constantly, cook over low heat 8 to 10 minutes until thickened and mixture coats a metal spoon. Remove from heat; cool to room temperature. Add remaining half and half, whipping cream and anise extract. Place frozen licorice in a heavy plastic bag. Using a meat mallet or hammer, crush licorice into small pieces. Do not add crushed licorice pieces to cream mixture until ready to freeze ice cream. Licorice pieces will dissolve if let stand for a long period in unfrozen cream mixture and *chip* effect will be lost. Add crushed licorice to cream mixture. Pour into ice-cream canister. *Immediately* freeze in ice-cream maker according to manufacturer's directions. *Complete now or make ahead.*

To complete now, store in home freezer 1 to 3 hours until mixture is firm. To serve, arrange in a large box with several other frozen desserts. Surround with ice and salt as directed on page 148. Dip ice-cream dipper into cold water before scooping individual servings. Serve in small bowls or sherbet dishes.

To make ahead, store frozen ice cream in home freezer up to 4 days. Serve as directed above. Makes about 2 quarts.

●●●

Strawberry-Banana Frozen Yogurt

Unique flavor combination with universal appeal.

16 oz. plain yogurt (2 cups)
1/2 teaspoon vanilla extract
3/4 cup sugar

3 cups fresh strawberries
2 bananas, sliced
1/4 cup light corn syrup

In a large bowl, combine yogurt, vanilla and sugar. Stir until sugar dissolves; set aside. Wash strawberries; remove and discard caps. In a blender or food processor fitted with a metal blade, process prepared berries, bananas and corn syrup until berries are finely chopped; stir into yogurt mixture. Pour into ice-cream canister. Freeze in ice-cream maker according to manufacturer's directions. *Complete now or make ahead.*

To complete now, store in home freezer 1 to 3 hours until mixture is firm. To serve, arrange in a large box with several other frozen desserts. Surround with ice and salt as directed on page 148. Dip ice-cream dipper into cold water before scooping individual servings. Serve in small bowls or sherbet dishes.

To make ahead, store frozen mixture in home freezer up to 4 days. Serve as directed above. Makes about 2 quarts.

How to Make Licorice-Chip Ice Cream

1/Gradually stir about 1 cup milk mixture into beaten egg yolks.

2/Using a meat mallet or hammer, break frozen licorice into small pieces.

Melba Sauce

A refreshing and versatile sauce to use on ice cream, waffles and fresh fruit.

1 (12-oz.) pkg, frozen unsweetened red raspberries or 3 cups fresh red raspberries	1/2 cup sugar 2 teaspoons cornstarch

Thaw berries if frozen. In a blender or food processor fitted with a metal blade, puree berries. Strain puree through 2 thicknesses of damp cheesecloth or a fine sieve to remove seeds; discard seeds. In a 1-quart saucepan, combine sugar and cornstarch; stir in raspberry puree. Stirring constantly, cook over low heat 4 to 5 minutes until mixture thickens slightly. Cool to room temperature. *Complete now or make ahead.*

To complete now, pour into a small serving dish. Refrigerate 2 hours or until thoroughly chilled.

To make ahead, pour into a container with a tight-fitting lid; refrigerate up to 3 days. Serve as directed above. Makes about 1-1/2 cups.

Peanut-Fudge Sauce

Photo on page 151.

A creamy smooth topping that's ideal for most mild-flavored and nut ice creams.

1-1/2 cups sugar
1/4 teaspoon salt
1/2 pint milk or half and half (1 cup)
1 tablespoon butter or margarine

3 oz. semisweet chocolate, chopped
1/2 cup chunk-style peanut butter
1/2 teaspoon vanilla extract

In a medium saucepan, combine sugar, salt and milk or half and half; stir until blended. Add butter or margarine and chocolate. Cook over low heat, stirring occasionally, until sugar dissolves and butter and chocolate melt. Simmer 5 to 6 minutes. Stir in peanut butter until melted and blended. Remove from heat; stir in vanilla. Cool to room temperature. *Complete now or make ahead.*

To complete now, pour into a small serving dish.

To make ahead, pour into a container with a tight-fitting lid; refrigerate up to 1 month. To serve, bring to room temperature. Serve as directed above. Makes about 2 cups.

● ● ●

Marbled Maple Sauce

Great as an ice-cream topping and terrific on French toast.

1/2 cup Reese's Pieces® candies
1/2 cup maple syrup

1/4 cup orange juice
1/8 teaspoon ground cinnamon

Pour candies into a heavy plastic bag; place bag in freezer or refrigerator to chill about 30 minutes. Place bag on a hard surface. Gently strike chilled candies with a wooden mallet to coarsely crack but not mash them. Set cracked candies aside. In a small saucepan, combine maple syrup, orange juice and cinnamon. Stirring constantly, cook over medium heat until mixture comes to a boil. Set aside to cool 5 minutes. *Complete now or make ahead.*

To complete now, pour syrup into a small serving dish. Add broken candies; *do not stir* or candy coating will dissolve. Arrange so all candy pieces are submerged in syrup. Cool to room temperature; gently stir once. Serve immediately.

To make ahead, pour into a container with a tight-fitting lid. Add broken candies; *do not stir* or candy coating will dissolve. Arrange so all candy pieces are submerged in syrup. When cooled to room temperature, gently stir once. Refrigerate up to 3 weeks. To serve, gently pour into a small serving dish. Let come to room temperature. Makes about 1 cup.

Orange-Pecan Topping

If served as a snack, use pecan halves; as a dessert topping, pecan pieces are best.

5 tablespoons brown sugar
1/2 teaspoon ground cinnamon
1/4 teaspoon ground nutmeg

1-1/2 cups pecan pieces or halves
1/3 cup orange juice

Preheat oven to 350F (175C). In a small bowl, combine 2 tablespoons brown sugar, 1/4 teaspoon cinnamon and 1/8 teaspoon nutmeg. Spread over bottom of an ungreased 9-inch-square baking pan. In same small bowl, combine remaining brown sugar, cinnamon and nutmeg; set aside. In another small bowl, combine pecans and orange juice. Stir until all nuts are wet. Pour nut mixture into a sieve to drain off excess orange juice. Spread wet nuts over brown-sugar mixture in pan. Sprinkle with reserved brown-sugar mixture. Bake in preheated oven 25 minutes, stirring at least twice. Spread on foil to cool. *Complete now or make ahead.*

To complete now, spoon cooled mixture into a small serving dish.

To make ahead, spoon into a container with a tight-fitting lid. Store at room temperature up to 3 weeks. Serve as directed above. Makes 1-1/2 cups.

— ●● —

Tropics Fruit & Nut Mix

Lends a taste of the tropics to your frozen dessert.

5 tablespoons sugar
1 teaspoon ground ginger
1/3 cup slivered almonds
1/3 cup shaved coconut

1/3 cup raisins
1/3 cup chopped dried papaya or
   dried apricots
1/3 cup pineapple juice

Spread 2 tablespoons sugar over bottom of a 9-inch-square baking pan. Sprinkle 1/2 teaspoon ginger over top. Preheat oven to 350F (175C). In a small bowl, combine almonds, coconut, raisins, papaya or apricots and pineapple juice; stir well. Pour mixture into a sieve to drain off excess pineapple juice. Spread coated mixture over sugar mixture in pan. Top with remaining 3 tablespoons sugar and 1/2 teaspoon ginger. Bake in preheated oven 25 minutes or until almonds begin to brown, stirring at least twice. Spread on foil to cool. When cooled, separate any clusters of mixture. *Complete now or make ahead.*

To complete now, spoon cooled mixture into a small serving dish.

To make ahead, place in a container with a tight-fitting lid; store at room temperature up to 3 weeks. Serve as directed above. Makes about 1-1/2 cups.

Index

Metric Chart

Comparison to Metric Measure

When You Know	Symbol	Multiply By	To Find	Symbol
teaspoons	tsp	5.0	milliliters	ml
tablespoons	tbsp	15.0	milliliters	ml
fluid ounces	fl. oz.	30.0	milliliters	ml
cups	c	0.24	liters	l
pints	pt.	0.47	liters	l
quarts	qt.	0.95	liters	l
ounces	oz.	28.0	grams	g
pounds	lb.	0.45	kilograms	kg
Fahrenheit	F	5/9 (after subtracting 32)	Celsius	C

Liquid Measure to Milliliters

1/4 teaspoon	=	1.25 milliliters
1/2 teaspoon	=	2.5 milliliters
3/4 teaspoon	=	3.75 milliliters
1 teaspoon	=	5.0 milliliters
1-1/4 teaspoons	=	6.25 milliliters
1-1/2 teaspoons	=	7.5 milliliters
1-3/4 teaspoons	=	8.75 milliliters
2 teaspoons	=	10.0 milliliters
1 tablespoon	=	15.0 milliliters
2 tablespoons	=	30.0 milliliters

Liquid Measure to Liters

1/4 cup	=	0.06 liters
1/2 cup	=	0.12 liters
3/4 cup	=	0.18 liters
1 cup	=	0.24 liters
1-1/4 cups	=	0.3 liters
1-1/2 cups	=	0.36 liters
2 cups	=	0.48 liters
2-1/2 cups	=	0.6 liters
3 cups	=	0.72 liters
3-1/2 cups	=	0.84 liters
4 cups	=	0.96 liters
4-1/2 cups	=	1.08 liters
5 cups	=	1.2 liters
5-1/2 cups	=	1.32 liters

Fahrenheit to Celsius

F	C
200—205	95
220—225	105
245—250	120
275	135
300—305	150
325—330	165
345—350	175
370—375	190
400—405	205
425—430	220
445—450	230
470—475	245
500	260